Airliners
of the
1970s

Gerry Manning

MIDLAND
An imprint of
Ian Allan Publishing

Airliners of the 1970s
© 2005 Gerry Manning

ISBN 1 85780 213 6

Published by Midland Publishing
4 Watling Drive, Hinckley, LE10 3EY, England
Tel: 01455 254 490 Fax: 01455 254 495
E-mail: midlandbooks@compuserve.com

Midland Publishing is an imprint of
Ian Allan Publishing Ltd

Worldwide distribution (except North America):
Midland Counties Publications
4 Watling Drive, Hinckley, LE10 3EY, England
Telephone: 01455 254 450 Fax: 01455 233 737
E-mail: midlandbooks@compuserve.com
www.midlandcountiessuperstore.com

North American trade distribution:
Specialty Press Publishers & Wholesalers Inc.
39966 Grand Avenue, North Branch, MN 55056
Tel: 651 277 1400 Fax: 651 277 1203
Toll free telephone: 800 895 4585
www.specialtypress.com

Design concept and layout
© 2005 Midland Publishing

Printed in England
by Ian Allan Printing Ltd
Riverdene Business Park, Molesey Road,
Hersham, Surrey, KT12 4RG

Title page photograph:

Spanish holiday charter carrier **Aviaco** were
operating Douglas DC-8-52 EC-ATP (c/n
45658) at Palma, Majorca in November 1974.
Having started life on the transatlantic services
of parent company Iberia, this aircraft later
became a Spanish air force VIP transport. The
airline was merged into its parent company in
September 1999.

Introduction

The aim of this book is to try to illustrate the range of both airlines
and airliners that operated during the decade of the 1970s. It
cannot of course be complete as it is of a limited size. It was
arguably one of the most significant decades in civil aviation's
history. It was the decade of the vast, with the introduction of the
widebody airliners. It was the decade of the fast, with the
introduction of the supersonic airliners. And yet it could still have
echoes from a gentler past, with four-engine flying boats still
operating.

I have attempted to make as wide a choice of types as possible
and at as many locations as possible. Some of the types were
financial disasters for their makers as they failed to sell in any
numbers which yet other types are still in production to this day.

With the captions I have attempted to note who the airline was,
or still is, what the aeroplane type was, and where and when
the picture was taken. Finally I outline the fate of the individual
aircraft.

Compared to these days of high-security and enthusiast-
unfriendly airports the decade of the 1970s was a different world.
Most airports still had excellent public viewing balconies and
permission for ramp access was possible. Good days… sadly
never to return.

Acknowledgements

The task of picking the slides to use was a good excuse for me
to view and raid the collections of old friends. The hard job was
to deciding what was not going to be used. My thanks for pictures
go to Bob O'Brien, Ken Fielding, Ian Keast, John Smith and Steve
Williams. Pictures without a credit are my own. Thanks also to Bill
Hodgson of Aerodata for filling in some gaps as to the fates of
various aircraft.

Gerry Manning
Liverpool

First flown in May 1950, the de Havilland Heron was an enlarged development of the DH.104 Dove. It was powered by four de Havilland Gipsy Queen piston engines of 250hp each. The type's role was as a feeder-liner for busy hubs and as a small airliner in its own right. Other uses included executive travel for a company with its own aeroplane. Pictured at London-Gatwick in August 1973 is de Havilland DH.114 Heron 1B 9L-LAD (c/n 14025) undergoing maintenance. It is operated by **Sierra Leone Airways**. This small west African carrier was based in the capital Freetown. Operations were suspended in 1987. This Heron was sold on to several operators and withdrawn and broken up for spares at Biggin Hill, Kent at the end of 1978. (John Smith)

The Heron 2 was a natural development and featured a retractable undercarriage. Due to less drag it gave better fuel economy and a 20mph speed advantage. Pictured at the company base of San Luis Obispo, California in October 1979 is de Havilland Heron 2B N414SA (c/n 14056) of **Swift Aire**. This carrier flew commuters around the state and had at one point over 100 daily departures; however, operations ceased in September 1981. This aircraft was a Riley Aeronautics Corporation conversion and had been re-engined with Lycoming IO-540s. It was sold to an operator in Fiji and crashed in December 1986.

The last passenger four-engined flying boats were operated by **Antilles Air Boats** based at St Croix in the Virgin Islands. The company was owned by Charles Blair who was a great pioneer in the field of navigation. In 1951 he flew a P-51 Mustang over the North Pole from Bardufoss in Norway to Fairbanks, Alaska. Short S.25 Sandringham VP-LVE (c/n SB 2018) is pictured on Lough Derg, Killaloe in the west of Ireland in August 1977. The Sandringham was a civil conversion of the World War Two Sunderland. It was operating pleasure flights to the Arran Islands. This aircraft is now preserved in a museum at Southampton in the UK and the airline was re-named Virgin Island Seaplane Shuttle in 1981.

The Bristol 170 Freighter was first flown in December 1945 as an all-purpose cargo aircraft. Its most famous role was as a car carrier across the English Channel. The Mk 31 carried two cars and their passengers and then came the Mk 32 Superfreighter. This had a nose extension of 5ft (1.524m) and carried a third vehicle. Pictured at the Lydd, Kent base of **British Air Ferries** in May 1970 is G-AMLP (c/n 13078) a Mk 32 converted from a short nose variant. The combination of hovercraft and fast ferries saw the demise of the car-across-the-Channel service. This aircraft was sold in Canada and crashed in March 1977.

The Aviation Traders Carvair was developed as a successor to the Bristol Freighter to operate long-haul car ferry services. The idea was from the managing director of Air Charter, the well known Mr Freddie Laker. He suggested taking a Douglas DC-4, cutting off the nose and replacing it with a new bulbous nose section featuring a front loading cargo door. Seen at Southend in May 1972 is ATL-98 Carvair G-AOFW (c/n 12/10351) of **British Air Ferries**. The carrier was re-named British World Airlines in 1993. This aircraft was broken up and scrapped at Southend at the end of 1983.

First flown in June 1965 the Britten Norman BN-2 Islander was a 9/10-seat utility aircraft with a fixed undercarriage and simple systems to aid maintenance at remote locations. Power was provided by a pair of 260hp Lycoming O-540 piston engines. I-TRAM (c/n 8) of Florence, Italy-based carrier **Aertirrena** is seen at Ford in August 1970. This third-level airline operated until 1975, and the aircraft can now be found in service with a carrier in the Dominican Republic.

One of the great workhorse props of the world has been the Curtiss C-46 Commando. It has the same layout as the Douglas C-47 but is a much larger machine. It can now only be found in places like Alaska, Bolivia and Colombia, all in declining numbers. C-46F N1651M (c/n 22399) of **Fairbanks Air Service** is pictured at Van Nuys, California in October 1976. The airline changed its name to Great Northern Airlines and this airframe can still be found today plying its trade as a flying fuel tanker in Alaska. Its role is to deliver fuel and oil to remote settlements and mining sites. (Steve Williams)

Until their sad demise in March 2001, **Reeve Aleutian Airways** of Anchorage, Alaska provided a passenger and cargo service to many small sites in America's largest state. Pictured at Anchorage in May 1977 is Curtiss C-46A Commando N9852F (c/n 26792). The fate of this aircraft is not known. (Bob O'Brien)

Flying that most elegant of airliners, the Lockheed Constellation, was French airline **Catair (Compagnie d'Affretements et de Transports Aériens)**. The carrier flew both cargo and passenger charters from 1968 until operations ceased in 1978. L-1049C Super Constellation F-BRAD (c/n 4519) is seen landing at Paris-Le Bourget in June 1971. This airframe has been preserved at Chateau Bougon Airport, Nantes and has been designated an 'Historical Monument' by the French government. (John Smith)

De Havilland Canada have had a long and well-deserved reputation for building rugged go-anywhere aircraft with excellent short-field performance. In the mid 1960s they produced the DHC-6 Twin Otter commuter aircraft. It had a high wing, fixed undercarriage, and power was provided by a pair of Pratt & Whitney PT-6A turboprops of 578shp. Over 800 aircraft were built. Pictured at Oakland, California in October 1979 is DHC-6-300 N127AP (c/n 289) of **Air Pacific**, a commuter operator based at Eureka. The following year the carrier merged with Gem State Airlines and this aircraft can be found today in Papua New Guinea flying for a missionary fellowship.

With a large number of lakes and harbours in British Columbia it was only natural for many aircraft to be fitted with floats to operate at downtown harbours. DHC-6 Twin Otter 200 C-FAIV (c/n 215) of **Airwest Airlines** is pictured at Victoria, Vancouver Island in July 1974. The Twin Otter was the largest aircraft operated by the Vancouver-based commuter carrier. Airwest were merged into Air BC in 1980, whilst the pictured aircraft crashed at Coal Harbour in September 1978.
(Ken Fielding)

The Short SC.7 Skyvan can trace its roots to the Miles Aerovan. The Skyvan had a very simple box-like fuselage with high wings, fixed undercarriage and a tail-loading facility. First flown in 1963, production aircraft were powered by a pair of Turboméca Astazou turboprops and then later by the more successful Garrett AiResearch TPE-331 with a power output of 715shp. Pictured at Mykonos, Greece in June 1975 is Skyvan 2 SX-BBO (c/n SH1870) operated by the Greek national carrier **Olympic Airways**. The Skyvan was used for short-haul passenger flights as well as freight on the carrier's inter-island operations. This aircraft can today be found in Sweden where it is operated by a Gothenburg-based parachute club for its members to jump from. (Ken Fielding)

Following the success of the Skyvan, Shorts of Belfast developed a 30-seater twin-engined commuter aircraft. This was the Shorts 330. It was less box-like but still simple. It did however feature a retractable undercarriage. Pictured at Santa Barbara, California in October 1979 is N330GW (c/n SH3010) of Los Angeles-based **Golden West Airlines**. This commuter carrier ceased operations in 1983. The aircraft was later sold to the US Army and adopted a military serial. (John Smith)

The Potez 840 was another type that changed powerplants early in its very limited production run. The design, a 16- to 24-seat commuter, was the last design from the firm of Henri Potez before it was taken over by Sud-Aviation. Potez 841 D-CHEF (c/n 2) of **Hertie** is seen at Düsseldorf in July 1970. Only six aircraft flew, including two prototypes. This aircraft was sold in the USA and was later retired and believed scrapped.

Designed for STOL (short take-off and landing) operations, the de Havilland DHC -7 Dash 7 was powered by four P&W PT6A turboprops of 1120shp each. It was able to operate from runways as short as 2,000ft (610m) using steep approach and climb-out with a low noise level. N9058P (c/n 5) of **Air Pacific** is seen at Bakersfield, California in October 1979. The carrier merged with Gem State and this aircraft can be found still in service in Venezuela.

Originally designed by Handley Page, the Jetstream was taken over by British Aerospace and developed into a very successful commuter by its Prestwick, Scotland factory. Handley Page Jetstream Mk.1 N666AE (c/n 213) of **Apollo Airways** is seen at Santa Barbara, California in October 1979. This carrier was renamed Pacific Coast and the aircraft was withdrawn from use at this airport and scrapped at the end of the 1980s. (John Smith)

Embraer of Brazil is now one of the world's leading producers of commuter and short-range jets. Its first design was the EMB-110 Bandeirante; nearly 500 aircraft were produced for both the civil and military markets. VH-MWV (c/n 110190) is operated by Australian carrier **Masling Commuter Services** based at Cootamundra, NSW. It is pictured at Melbourne-Essendon in November 1978. The carrier was renamed Wings Australia following its purchase by Jet Charter Airlines in 1981. The aircraft is still in Australia and is operated by a sports parachute company in Brisbane. (Bob O'Brien)

LACSA (Lineas Aéreas Costarricanses S A) was the flag carrier for the Central American republic of Costa Rica: they now operate as TACA Costa Rica. Douglas DC-6A TI-LRC (c/n 45059) was operated by the cargo division of the company. It is pictured at Miami in August 1976. The aircraft was sold to the Mexican Air Force and has since been withdrawn from service and stored at Mexico City. (Bob O'Brien)

A small number of Douglas DC-6s were converted to have swing-tails to facilitate the loading of irregular-shaped or long items of cargo. One such aircraft was DC-6B OH-KDA (c/n 45202) operated by Finnish carrier Kar-Air. It is seen on a visit to Manchester in May 1979. Kar-Air was owned by the national flag carrier Finnair who absorbed them into the main carrier in May 1996. This aircraft was sold to an American cargo carrier in 1982 and destroyed by fire following a landing accident in Alaska in September 2001. (John Smith)

Belgian charter carrier Delta Air Transport was based at Antwerp. They were a passenger charter carrier with a fleet of DC-3s and DC-6s who were taken over by the then flag carrier Sabena. Pictured at Luton in September 1973 on a football charter, is Douglas DC-6B OO-RVG (c/n 43549). The aircraft can be found today in the care of the world's largest operator of this classic propliner, Northern Air Cargo of Alaska. (John Smith)

Once owned by the Somoza family, who ruled the country until the 1979 revolution, **LANICA (Lineas Aereas de Nicaragua)** was based in the capital Managua. The carrier had been set up with the help of Pan Am in 1945 and was declared insolvent in March 1981. Pictured having a car loaded into its freight door at Miami in August 1976 is Douglas DC-6B AN-BFN (c/n 45322). This aircraft crashed in West Virginia in June 1979. It is of note that the registration letters for Nicaragua have since changed from 'AN' to 'YN'. (Bob O'Brien)

Arriving at London-Gatwick from Palma in August 1970, DC-6B EC-BBK (c/n 44434) of Spantax is typical of the 'hand-me-down' aircraft employed at the beginning of the decade by the expanding inclusive-tour sector. Its versatility increased in 1968 by a 'swing-tail' conversion not apparent here (the hinges are on the starboard side), this aircraft found further work as N434TA with Zantop and Northern Air Cargo. It was withdrawn from use at the turn of the century but still graced the Fairbanks apron in the summer of 2005. (Dave Peel)

Fort Lauderdale-based **Mackey International Airlines** was a general ad-hoc cargo carrier which ceased operations in 1981. Pictured at their Florida base in August 1976 is Douglas DC-6B N37579 (c/n 45131). This cargo-configured aircraft was sold on to a number of American operators and crashed in the Bahamas in 1984. (Bob O'Brien)

French charter operator **Trans-Union** was based in the south of the country at Marseille. In 1971 operations were transferred to Europe Aero Services. Pictured at Paris-Le Bourget in July 1970 is Douglas DC-6B F-BNUZ (c/n 45173). This aircraft was used to fly a nightly newspaper contract for Air France. It was damaged beyond repair following a heavy landing at Nice in October 1971 and broken up at the end of that year.

The last of a long line of Douglas piston-engined airliners, the DC-7 was the ultimate in technology when it was launched in 1953. The arrival of jets and turboprops made its life with the main carriers relatively short. It went onto, and still does, have a role in cargo and fire-fighting operations. Pictured at Palma-Majorca in January 1972 are a pair of DC-7Cs of **Spantax**, a Spanish holiday charter carrier. EC-BBT (c/n 45553) was retired and stored at Las Palmas, Canary Islands in 1976 and has since 1979 been seen by a motorway on the island in increasingly poor condition. EC-ATR (c/n 45309) was withdrawn in January 1977 and broken up at Madrid during that year. Spantax operated from 1959 until services were suspended in March 1988. (John Smith)

Douglas DC-7C VR-BCX (c/n 45310) of **ARCO Bermuda** is pictured at Rotterdam in July 1970. It is operating a cargo service to the UK during a dock workers' strike; note it does not have a cargo door. The carrier suspended services the following year. The aircraft was sold on and then seized by the Swiss authorities at Basel in March 1971. It was broken up at this location in 1980.

The Martin 4-0-4 was developed from the company's earlier model, the 2-0-2. It was a modern pressurised tricycle-undercarriage airliner to restock the airlines of America following World War Two. Its main competitor was the Convair 240/340/440 range. Pictured at Opa Locka, Florida in July 1974 is N967M (c/n 14149) of **Marco Island Airways**, a local service passenger carrier. They were taken over by PBA (Provincetown-Boston Airline) in 1984. This airframe was retired and stored at Naples, Florida in November 1984 and broken up in 1995. (Steve Williams)

Pictured at the company base of Atlanta, Georgia in July 1974 is **Southern Airways** Martin 4-0-4 N149S (c/n 14141). Southern had been formed in 1949 and grew to cover many states. In 1979 they merged with North Central to form Republic. The aeroplane joined the Mid-Atlantic Air Museum in Reading PA in 1991 and has been painted in the livery of Eastern Airlines, the first operator of this aircraft in 1952. It is airworthy. (Steve Williams)

It is unlikely for many years to come that any decade of aviation will not feature the Douglas DC-3. Many 'DC-3 replacements' have come and gone and the only true replacement has proved to be another DC-3! Pictured at Lympne, Kent in May 1970 is G-AMWW (c/n 33010) of **Skyways Air Cargo**. This company was part of the Skyways group and operated scheduled cargo services to Belgium and France. The carrier suspended services in 1980. This aircraft was sold in America and converted by Basler at Oshkosh to turboprop power. It is now owned by the Colombian Air Force.

Australian carrier **Forrestair Cargo** flew services from Melbourne across the Bass Strait to Tasmania. Operations ceased in November 1978. Douglas DC-3 VH-TAK (c/n 13338) is photographed at Melbourne-Essendon in December 1979. The aircraft has been scrapped and the cockpit is on display at a museum in Bendigo, Victoria. (Bob O'Brien)

Pictured at the company base of Melbourne-Essendon in December 1979 is Douglas DC-3 VH-BAB (c/n 25495) of **BBA Cargo** (Brain & Brown Airfreighters). It was during this month that the company ceased operations. This aircraft has been preserved at the Air World Museum, Wangaratta, Victoria in military colours. (Bob O'Brien)

Frontier Flying Services of Fairbanks Alaska currently operates a modern fleet of Beech commuter liners for passenger services around the state. The largest aircraft in the fleet has been Douglas DC-3 N59314 (c/n 12363). It is pictured at Ryan Field, Arizona in October 1979. Sold on, it is currently in store at Palmer, Alaska.

Kestrel Airways was formed in 1970 with a single aircraft. Operations were ad-hoc passenger and freight charters. Douglas DC-3 G-AMFV (c/n 10105) is pictured at East Midlands-Castle Donington in April 1971. Operations ceased in November of the following year. The aircraft was broken up for spares in August 1973.

Masling Commuter Services was an Australian carrier who operated a single DC-3 for charter work and newspaper deliveries. In 1981 they changed their name to Wings Australia. Pictured at Melbourne-Essendon in December 1979 is Douglas DC-3 VH-MWQ (c/n 9583). It is currently used for sports parachuting in Australia's Northern Territory. (Bob O'Brien)

Norwich-based Air Anglia was formed in 1970 by the merging of three local operators. Both charter and scheduled passenger services were flown. They became Air UK in 1980. Photographed on a charter at Liverpool-Speke in March 1973 is Douglas DC-3 G-AOBN (c/n 11711). The aircraft was sold on and ended its days in Ethiopia where it was destroyed on the ground at Jiggiga airfield in 1977.

British United formed **BUIA (British United Island Airways)** to cover services to the Channel Islands and the Isle of Man. The livery remained basic BUA. The carrier evolved into British Island Airways. Seen at London-Gatwick in July 1970 is Douglas DC-3 G-AMHJ (c/n 13468) operating cargo services. The aircraft remained operational until 2001 with Air Atlantique in a pollution control role. It was fitted with spray bars to combat oil spills around the UK coast.

From its formation in 1966 to being bought out in 1972, UK independent airline **South West Aviation** was based in Exeter. Operations were of a charter nature and included flying flowers from the Channel Islands. Photographed at Exeter in August 1970 is Douglas DC-3 G-AMYJ (c/n 32716). The airframe had a long career with Air Atlantique and has found a home preserved with the Yorkshire Air Museum at Elvington.

In 1943 Vultee Aircraft merged with Consolidated Aircraft to form Consolidated Vultee, four years later this was shortened to Convair. With the end of the war in sight it looked to build a new airliner. The 110 flew in 1946 but was considered too small. The 240 (2 engines/40 passengers) followed. A modern tricycle undercarriage airliner it was powered by a pair of Pratt & Whitney R-2800 radial piston engines of 2400hp each. Pictured at Woensdrecht, Holland in July 1970 is Convair CV-240 LN-KLT (c/n 310) of Norwegian carrier **Polaris Air Transport**. The airline flew passenger and cargo charters between 1966 and 1967 with a mix of Convairs and DC-3s. The airframe was scrapped in the mid 1970s.

Convair followed the -240 with the -340 and -440. They had a longer fuselage and wider wing span, up to 52 passengers could be carried. Convair CV-440 N30KA (c/n 364) of **Key Air Lines** is pictured at Oxnard, California in October 1979. Key flew scheduled cargo and passenger services around the western states as well as military contract work. They were taken over by Presidential and this aircraft was retired and broken up at Opa Locka, Florida in 1998.

Several of the main European flag carriers could still be found operating piston Convairs at the start of the decade. Convair CV-440 OH-LRE (c/n 400) of **Finnair** is seen at London-Gatwick in March 1970. This aircraft is still currently active as a cargo aircraft in the USA. (Ken Fielding)

Oslo, Norway-based **Nor-Fly** flew charter services, both passenger and freight, around western Europe until they merged with Partnair in 1985. Convair CV-440 LN-MAP (c/n 331) is pictured at Manchester in September 1978. This aircraft was withdrawn from use in 1982 and then used by Oslo Airport Fire Service for rescue practice. (John Smith)

Any new western airliner being developed in the 1960s was going to be powered by turboprops. Convair declined to develop the range so it was PacAero Engineering who pioneered the work, first with the short-lived Napier Eland and then with the Allison 501 delivering 3750shp. Such conversions became Convair CV-580s. N73153 (c/n 179) of **Sierra Pacific Airlines** is seen at Marana, Arizona in October 1979. This carrier currently operates a pair of Boeing 737s and this airframe has begun a new life as an aerial fire-fighter, being equipped with a belly tank for the suppression of forest fires in Canada.

One of the leading domestic carriers in the eastern states of the USA was **Allegheny Airlines**. At the end of the 1970s they took the operating name of US Air. Convair CV-580 N5833 (c/n 115) is pictured at New York-Newark in July 1970. This aircraft was sold in Canada, withdrawn from use in 1994 and then scrapped. (Steve Williams)

The Lockheed C-130 Hercules started production in 1954 and is still being built in a much updated form. There can be no other transport aircraft that has had an unbroken fifty-plus-year production history. Whilst the vast majority of the aircraft are for the air forces of the world some can be found in the hands of civil cargo operators. Pictured at Pensacola Naval Air Station, Florida in July 1974 is Lockheed L-100-30 N15ST (c/n 4391) of **Saturn Airways**. The company flew passenger charters to Europe for many years and merged with TIA at the end of 1976. This aircraft was destroyed in a take-off crash at Kelly Air Force Base, Texas in October 1986. (Steve Williams)

First flown in 1959, the Armstrong-Whitworth Argosy was designed as a large bulk capacity freighter. It had a high wing, twin booms and loading from both front and rear doors. Four Rolls-Royce Dart turboprops of 1910shp each provide the power. Pictured at Liverpool-Speke in September 1977 is Argosy 101 G-BEOZ (c/n 6660) of **Air Bridge Carriers**. Operations from Liverpool included daily newspaper flights. The company was renamed Hunting Cargo Airlines in 1993 and this aircraft has been preserved at East Midlands Airport since 1987. (Bob O'Brien)

The Argosy C.1 was developed for the RAF and had more powerful Dart engines with an output of 2680shp. The nose-opening door was deleted and the rear door was hinged to open upwards and downwards for in-flight drops. Following defence cuts at the start of the 1970s, the RAF transport fleet was retired and many were purchased for civil operations. One such was **ORAS – Otrag Range Air Services**. Its role was to support a rocket range in Zaïre. Argosy C.1 9Q-COA (c/n 6791) is seen, in its very distinctive colour scheme, at East Midlands-Castle Donington Airport in June 1978. It was stored at this location and broken up in 1981. (John Smith)

First flown in 1962, the NAMC (Nihon Aircraft Manufacturing Co) YS-11 was the first and only Japanese designed and built post-World War Two airliner. Power was from a pair of Rolls-Royce Dart turboprops of 3060shp each. As well as domestic sales it sold well to the USA together with countries such as Brazil and Greece. Total production was 182 including two prototypes. Pictured at Tokoyo-Haneda in May 1977 is YS-11A-217 JA8788 (c/n 2176) of **TOA Domestic Airlines**. This carrier was the first to operate the type in April 1965. In April 1988 the company changed its name to Japan Air System. The pictured aircraft has remained with the company, operated by the subsidiary Japan Air Commuter, until 2004. (Bob O'Brien)

Japan's second airline, **All Nippon Airways**, flies both domestic and long-haul passenger services. Pictured in an early colour scheme is NAMC YS-11A-208 JA8697 (c/n 2066) at Tokoyo-Haneda in May 1977. Sold in America it was retired and stored in 1991. (Bob O'Brien)

The 300 series of the YS-11 had a port side freight door and was a combi for mixed passenger and cargo services. YS-11A-307 N171RV (c/n 2071) of **Reeve Aleutian Airways** is at the company base of Anchorage, Alaska in July 1979. The carrier suspended operations in March 2001 and this aircraft is currently flying cargo services for a company in Mexico. (Bob O'Brien)

The Rolls-Royce Dart was the selected powerplant for the Avro/HS.748. This was one of several 'DC-3 replacements' designed at the end of the 1950s. HS.748 Series 1 G-ARMW (c/n 1537) of **Skyways** is seen at Manchester in June 1972 in the final livery of the British passenger carrier. During that year they were taken over by Dan-Air. The aircraft was sold in Nepal and was reported as derelict in Kathmandu at the end of 1999. (Ken Fielding)

Once the largest independent airline in Europe, **Dan-Air** had a history dating back to 1953 when it was formed by shipping brokers Davies and Newman. Following losses they were taken over by British Airways. HS.748 Series 2 G-BEBA (c/n 1613) is seen at the carrier's Lasham base in August 1976. Sold on to Canada it was destroyed by fire in Ontario in 1991. (John Smith)

National airline of the island chain of the Bahamas is **Bahamasair**; an airline founded in 1973. Pictured at their Nassau base in December 1979 is HS.748 Series 2A C6-BED (c/n 1763). This aircraft was damaged beyond economic repair by a hurricane at Nassau in October 1998 having previously been withdrawn from service. (Bob O'Brien)

The original Handley Page Herald was powered by four Alvis Leonides radial piston engines of 870hp each. In view of competition from other 'DC-3 replacements' it was re-engined with a pair of Rolls-Royce Dart turboprops of 2105shp each and first flown in this configuration in March 1958. It was not a great financial success, with a total production run of just fifty aircraft. HPR.7 Herald 202 G-BCZG (c/n 159) of **Air UK** is seen at Manchester in May 1979. This carrier was taken over by KLM to form KLM uk. The aircraft was sold to an airline in Zaïre and crashed in September 1984. (John Smith)

BIA (British Island Airways) evolved from BUIA and its role was to provide scheduled passenger services to the Channel Islands and the Isle of Man. Operations ceased in 1990. Handley Page HPR.7 Herald 209 G-BBXJ (c/n 196) is seen at Exeter in July 1974. In December of that year it was damaged beyond repair at Jersey and ended its days on the fire dump.

Air Ecosse was one of the marketing names used by Fairflight Charters for services in Scotland. In 1989 they ceased flight operations. HPR.7 Herald 209 G-BFRJ (c/n 195) is pictured at East Midlands-Castle Donington in June 1978. This aircraft was put on display on the viewing deck at London-Gatwick in 1996 but removed in 2003. (John Smith)

Like a number of airliners of the period, the Lockheed Electra had a relatively short front-line service as the public wanted pure jets. It did have a long secondary role as a passenger carrier, and in its cargo role still flies to this day. First flown in 1957, the four-engined aircraft was powered by Allison 501 turboprops of 3750shp and could carry up to 96 passengers. Pictured at Cleveland, Ohio in August 1970 is L-188C Electra N125US (c/n 1101) of **American Flyers Airline**. The carrier specialised in non-scheduled passenger charters for the US military. They were bought out by Universal Airlines in 1971. This aircraft was sold on to a number of different operators and was broken up at Miami in 1989. (Steve Williams)

Miami-based Eastern Airlines was the first company to put the Electra into commercial service, this being in January 1959. Pictured at New York-La Guardia in June 1976 is L-188A Electra N5517 (c/n 1023) operating the **Eastern Air-Shuttle**. The company suspended all services in January 1991, whilst this airframe was converted to a cargo carrier and destroyed by fire on the ground at Detroit-Willow Run in April 1993. (Bob O'Brien)

Australia's **Ansett-ANA** was one of the first operators of the Lockheed Electra, putting the first into service in March 1959. They converted their fleet to freighters in the 1970s and operated them until 1984. Ansett went out of business in 2001. L-188AF Electra VH-RMG (c/n 1123) is seen at Brisbane in November 1976. This aircraft was sold to the Argentine Navy in 1983. Following the Falklands/Malvinas conflict with the UK, Argentina was not able to obtain maritime patrol aircraft to replace its retired P-2 Neptunes. It decided to buy a number of Electras and convert them to *Explorador* standard with search radar and other maritime fitments. It should be remembered that the most widely used maritime patrol aircraft, the P-3 Orion, is also based upon the Electra. The pictured aircraft was destroyed in a non-fatal crash at Trelew in September 1989. (Bob O'Brien)

Evergreen International Airlines are based at Marana, Arizona and today have an all-jet fleet of DC-9 and Boeing 747 freighters. They operated Electras from 1975 to 1983. Pictured at Marana in October 1979 is L-188A Electra N5534 (c/n 1072). This airframe was also sold to the Argentine Navy and converted to a maritime patrol aircraft. In 1997 the American government decided to sell the P-3 Orion to Argentina and so the *Exploradores* were retired. The illustrated one is now preserved in the navy museum.

In the days before low-cost no-frills airlines the cost of flying was out of reach of many people. From this fact grew travel clubs where the members owned an airliner for their holiday travel. The Detroit-based **Nomads** were one such group. L-188C Electra N836E (c/n 2008) is at Marana, Arizona in October 1979. The group flew this aircraft from 1971 to 1981 before replacing it with a Boeing 727 that is operated to this day. The Electra was sold in Indonesia and destroyed by fire after a belly landing in November 1985.

With the success of the Viscount in commercial service, **BEA (British European Airways)** asked Vickers for a bigger and faster version for both domestic and European routes. First flown in January 1959 it was powered by four Rolls-Royce Tyne turboprops of 4985shp each. It did not have anything like the sales figures of the Viscount, selling just 43 to BEA and Trans Canada. BEA converted a number to Merchantman freighters by fitting stronger floors and a large cargo door. V.953 Vanguard/Merchantman G-APEL (c/n 715) of BEA is at Manchester in May 1972. Sold on to a number of operators it crashed at Toulouse in France in January 1988. (Ken Fielding)

Air Bridge Carriers were one of the second line of Vanguard operators and, in their new name of Hunting Cargo, the final operator of the type in the 1990s. Pictured at its East Midlands-Castle Donington base in October 1978 is V.953C Vanguard/ Merchantman G-APES (c/n 721). The aircraft was withdrawn from use at this location in 1995 and two years later broken up. The cockpit section was saved and is displayed at the local Aeropark.

Air Viking was a short-lived Icelandic holiday charter operator. It flew passengers from Keflavik to the southern European sunspots. Vickers V.952 Vanguard TF-AVA (c/n 727) is at Stansted in August 1970. The carrier ceased services at the end of that year. The aircraft was sold on to a number of operators and retired at Perpignan, France in July 1979, where it was subsequently broken up.

French carrier **Europe Aero Services** became one of the largest operators of both Vanguards and Merchantmen. Pictured at Paris-Le Bourget in June 1973 is V.952 Vanguard F-BTYB (c/n 734). The carrier flew holiday charters as well as a scheduled freight service on behalf of Air France. EAS operated Vanguards until 1981 and the company renamed itself EAS – Europe Airlines. The pictured aircraft, like most of the company's fleet, ended its days at their Perpignan base where it was broken up. (John Smith)

British holiday charter carrier **Invicta International** was founded in 1964 and in 1970 acquired their first Vanguard. A total of seven were operated either as passenger or freight configured. V.952 Vanguard G-AXOO (c/n 733) is pictured at Manchester in May 1972. The airline ceased passenger services in 1975 while this aircraft was withdrawn at Manston, Kent in May 1973 and broken up three years later. (Ken Fielding)

The Canadair CL-44 was based upon the Bristol Britannia, it being stretched and powered by Rolls-Royce Tyne turboprops. The first batch, for the Royal Canadian Air Force, were designated CC-106 Yukon. Following this was the CL-44D; this featured a swing-tail to ease loading of bulky cargo and long items. The production run of both only amounted to 39 aircraft. Pictured at North Weald in May 1972 is CL-44D4-2 G-AXAA (c/n 18) of **Transmeridian Air Cargo**. The carrier was renamed British Cargo Airlines in 1979 and the airframe was sold in America, withdrawn from service in 1988, and then broken up in 1999 at Greensboro, North Carolina.

Pictured at London-Gatwick in May 1972 is Canadair CL-44D4-1 G-AWOV (c/n 32) of UK cargo operator **Tradewinds**. This is a popular name for an airline as there have also been carriers in the USA and Singapore with this name. The UK company ceased operations in September 1990 and the illustrated aircraft ended its days in Tripoli, Libya, where it was broken up. (Steve Williams)

A single CL-44 was converted in 1969 by Conroy Aviation as an oversize cargo carrier with a bulbous fuselage. Its prime task was the transportation of Rolls-Royce RB211 engines to Lockheeds for the L-1011 TriStar. Conroy CL-44-O N447T (c/n 16) is pictured at Stansted in August 1970 operated by UK carrier **Transmeridian Air Cargo**. It is in storage today at Bournemouth-Hurn, UK, having passed through a number of owners.

Starting revenue services in 1971 Argentine cargo carrier **TAR – Transporte Aero Rioplatense** flew world-wide charters. Pictured climbing out of London-Gatwick in August 1973 is Canadair CL-44D4-6 LV-JTN (c/n 34). The carrier suspended services in 1989. This aircraft was destroyed in July 1981 whilst on a flight from Teheran to Cyprus, having reportedly delivered weapons to the Iranian government, who were in the midst of a war with Iraq at the time. It was returning empty when it strayed over the Soviet territory of Armenia. There were no survivors in the CL-44 and so the only account comes from the Russian fighter pilot who claims to have tried to get the aircraft to land and, when this failed, resorted to ramming it! Perhaps the real truth of why it was where it was and what happened will never be known. (John Smith)

Set up in 1975, **Transmeridian Hong Kong** operated a single aircraft taken from the parent company. It flew cargo services across Asia from the then British colony. Canadair CL-44D4-2 VR-HHC (c/n 17) is pictured at Stansted in May 1978. Sold on, it was eventually withdrawn and broken up at Greensboro, North Carolina in 1995. (John Smith)

First flown on Christmas Eve 1962 the Nord 262 was a pressurised version of the earlier 260. Its role was that of a 26/28-seat turboprop airliner and yet another aircraft striving to be the DC-3 replacement. UK carrier **Dan-Air** operated one for eighteen months in this role before it was supplanted by HS.748s. Nord 262A-22 G-AYFR (c/n 29) is pictured at Liverpool-Speke in May 1971. It was sold on to be operated in America and withdrawn and stored at the end of 1987.

Pictured on the ramp at Düsseldorf in July 1970 is Nord 262A-30 D-CADY (c/n 37). It is operated by **IFG Inter Regional**, a German domestic passenger carrier. This aircraft was sold in the USA, moved to South America and is currently in service in Guatemala, Central America.

The most successful of all the 'DC-3 replacements' has been the Dutch designed and built Fokker F.27 Friendship. It was first flown in 1955 and like all of its competitors was powered by a pair of Rolls-Royce Dart turboprops. Many can be found in service today in all parts of the world. It was later developed into a 'second-generation' aircraft, the Fokker 50; this having a glass cockpit and new powerplants. F-27-100 D-BAKI (c/n 10102) of German domestic passenger carrier **IFG Inter Regional** is seen on the ramp at Düsseldorf in July 1970. The airline had been set up by holiday charter company LTU in 1967 to cover scheduled services, IFG ceased operations in January 1974. This airframe was the second one built and has been preserved by the F-27 Friendship Association at Lelystad.

Pictured on the ramp at its home base of Nairobi in March 1977 is **Kenya Airways** Fokker F.27-200 5H-AAI (c/n 10213). This airline currently operates an all-Boeing fleet. The pictured aircraft was written off following a belly landing in July 1988. (Bob O'Brien)

Owned by Swissair, **Balair** was a leading holiday charter operator. They were merged with CTA in 1993 to form Balair CTA and two years later merged into the main company. Pictured at Geneva in July 1970 is Fokker F.27 Friendship 200 HB-AAV (c/n 10276). The aircraft was sold on to a number of different operators and retired from use in Argentina in 1996, where it is now derelict.

French flag carrier **Air France** used a fleet of Friendships to carry post around the country. Photographed at Beauvais in May 1971 is Fokker F.27-500 F-BSUO (c/n 10449). This aircraft is still plying its trade around the skies of Europe with a Dutch airline.

Gulf Air is the multinational airline for the states of Bahrain, Oman and Abu Dhabi. They currently operate an all-jet fleet of the latest Airbus and Boeing designs. Pictured on the ramp at Bahrain in September 1977 is Fokker F.27-600 Friendship A4O-FA (c/n 10443). This aircraft was used on lease for several years and spent the rest of its life with European carriers before being destroyed in a crash at Hanover, Germany in May 1988. (Bob O'Brien)

Pictured on the manufacturer's ramp at Amsterdam-Schiphol is **TAA – Trans Australia Airlines** Fokker F.27-600 PH-EXB (c/n 10441), prior to delivery as VH-TQS in July 1970. The carrier was renamed Australian Airlines in 1986 and this aircraft was sold in Indonesia in 1997 and retired in 2003.

American manufacturer Fairchild took out a licence with Fokker to build the Friendship in the USA. The prototype first flew in April 1958. Over 200 F-27s and stretched FH-227s were built at their Hagerstown, Maryland, factory. Pictured in store at Marana, Arizona in October 1979 is Fairchild F-27 HK-1137 (c/n 40) of **TAC Colombia** (Transportes Aéreas de Cesar). The carrier flew domestic passenger services and in 1980 changed their name to Aerocesar. This aircraft migrated to Europe and operated in Denmark as a freighter until it was retired in August 2001 at Billund.

The Vickers Viscount was the most successful turboprop airliner of its generation with a total of 445 aircraft built including prototypes. They were sold the world over and continued to serve into the new millennium. Power was supplied by four Rolls-Royce Dart turboprops. Pictured at Prestwick in October 1976 is Viscount 814 G-BAPG (c/n 344) in the colours of **British Airways**, they had leased the aircraft from British Midland. The airframe was withdrawn from use at Southend in 1992 and broken up five years later.

BEA **(British European Airways)** had one of the largest fleets of Viscounts. Pictured with extra 'Channel Islands' titles at Manchester in August 1972 is Viscount 802 G-AOHR (c/n 166). It was withdrawn at Cardiff in 1975 and broken up the following year. (Bob O'Brien)

Owned by British Midland, this Viscount 815 was leased to short-lived UK independent carrier **Kestrel International Airways**. G-AVJB (c/n 375) is pictured at Manchester in June 1972. The aircraft has been preserved in a theme park in Sweden. (Ken Fielding)

Originally known as Derby Airways, and now as bmi, **British Midland** have a long history as a scheduled passenger carrier. Pictured at the company base of East Midlands-Castle Donington in July 1978, is Viscount 838 G-BCZR (c/n 446). This aircraft was sold on to an African operator, retired in 1990, and reported derelict by 1996. (John Smith)

British independent passenger carrier **Alidair** operated many services in support of the oil industry off the Scottish North Sea coast. Pictured at Manchester in August 1972 is Viscount 812 G-AVJL (c/n 389). The carrier changed its name to Inter City Airlines in 1981. The aircraft was sold in Indonesia and written off in October 1983 at Semerang. (Ken Fielding)

From its start in Wales in 1935, **Cambrian Airways** grew to be a major independent British scheduled passenger carrier with extensive domestic routes. They were absorbed into British Airways in 1972. Viscount 806 G-AOYJ (c/n 259) is at Liverpool-Speke in April 1971. This airframe was sold on and was retired at Southend in 1993. It was broken up there three years later. (Ken Fielding)

Northeast Airlines was the new name for BKS Air Transport. It reflected the area of the UK that it served best. The company was later merged into British Airways. Viscount 806 G-APEY (c/n 382) is pictured at Manchester in June 1972. This aircraft was sold in Africa and reported as being destroyed in an accident in 2004. (Ken Fielding)

Channel Airways flew both scheduled services as well as holiday charters. They took that name in 1956 and operated until 1972 when services were suspended. Pictured at the carrier's Southend base in May 1972 is Vickers Viscount 812 G-AVNJ (c/n 361). The aircraft was broken up the following month.

The elegant Bristol Britannia was one of the turboprop airliners that arrived only a short time before the pure jets came into service. First flown in 1952, the type entered service with BOAC (British Overseas Airways Corporation) in 1956. It went on to have a long life flying with the holiday charter operators or, in the case of ex-RAF machines, on cargo services. Britannia 305 G-ANCE (c/n 12921) of **Lloyd International** is at Liverpool-Speke in June 1970. This company operated passenger and cargo services to Africa and the Far East as well as holiday charters; it ceased operations in June 1972. The pictured aircraft was sold on and was finally retired at Dublin in 1979, being broken up two years later. (Steve Williams)

British holiday charter operator **Monarch Airlines** was founded in 1967 and currently operates a mixed fleet of Airbus and Boeing designs. Bristol Britannia 312 G-AOVH (c/n 12925) is seen at the company's Luton base in September 1970. It was withdrawn from service the following year and used as a cabin crew trainer before being broken up in 1972. (Steve Williams)

Donaldson International Airways was another British holiday charter carrier. It operated four Britannias and ceased trading in 1974. Britannia 312 G-AOVF (c/n 13237) was at Coventry in August 1972. This aircraft can be seen today preserved at the RAF Museum at Cosford in the livery of BOAC, the first operator of this airframe. (Bob O'Brien)

Founded in 1966 **Air Spain** was a Spanish carrier which brought northern European holidaymakers to the country's resorts; they ceased operations at the start of 1975. Britannia 312 EC-BSY (c/n 13421) is pictured at Brussels in August 1970. It was sold on and finally retired in Zaïre in 1991 where it was broken up.

Founded in 1966 **Air Spain** was a Spanish carrier who brought northern European holidaymakers to the country's resorts; they ceased operations at the start of 1975. Britannia 312 EC-BSY (c/n 13421) is pictured at Brussels in August 1970. It was sold on and finally ceased flying in Zaïre in 1991 where it was broken up.

AMAZ (Agence et Messageries Aérienne du Zaïre) of Kinshasa bought this former RAF Britannia 253 9Q-CAJ (c/n 13511) in November of 1975. The deal did not go through and it was not delivered. It is pictured at Luton in September 1976. The airframe found a role as an engine test-bed before being scrapped in 1980. (John Smith)

Operating a single ex-RAF Britannia 253 was **Interconair** (Irish Intercon Cattle Meats). Pictured at Luton in April 1976 is EI-BBY (c/n 13455) in a livery that reveals its former military roots. It was written off following a landing accident at Shannon in September 1977.

Irish cargo carrier **Aer Turas** operated from 1962 until 2003. They flew a wide range of cargo aircraft from a Bristol Freighter to a Lockheed TriStar. Bristol Britannia 253 EI-BBH (c/n 13436) is pictured arriving at Liverpool-Speke in November 1979. This aircraft was sold in Zaïre during 1981, being withdrawn from use and broken up in 1992. (Both John Smith)

To operate a service between Lisbon and Luanda in Angola, Portuguese carrier **Eurafric** bought Bristol Britannia 253 EI-BCI (c/n 13449). The aircraft was delivered to Lisbon but no revenue services were flown and it did not take up a Portuguese registration. It was then leased to Aer Turas. Its days ended, as for so many of the type, in Zaïre. It was sold there in 1982, retired and broken up four years later. It is pictured at Luton in May 1978. (John Smith)

Based in Dubai (UAE), **Air Faisal** flew services to Bombay and other cities in India. They obtained their first Britannia in November 1975 and a second followed in February 1977, services closed down in 1979. Britannia 253 G-BEMZ (c/n 13457) is seen at Luton in May 1978. It was sold to Zaïre in 1981, withdrawn and broken up in 1992. (John Smith)

Young Air Cargo was based in Belgium at Gosselies. The carrier was set up in 1975 and ceased operations in 1979. Pictured at Stansted in August 1976 is Britannia 253 XM497/OO-YCF (c/n 13509). This aircraft was purchased for spares to supply the operational fleet of four. It is still in basic RAF markings.

Douglas, who became McDonnell Douglas in April 1967, developed the DC-9 for the growing jet-powered, short-haul market following on the sales success of the Caravelle and BAC One-Eleven. They became masters of the market by being able to stretch the fuselage over the years as the demand for more seats grew. The base line DC-9-10 series started at 104ft (31.7m) long and was the first model into service. Pictured at Palma-Majorca in November 1974 is DC-9-14 EC-CGY (c/n 45696) of Spanish holiday charter carrier **Spantax**. The company was formed in October 1959 to fly oil contracts in Spanish Morocco and ceased operations in 1988. This aircraft, the second built, was sold in America and stayed in service with Midwest Express until 2004. (John Smith)

British Midland used its DC-9s for domestic and European passenger services. Douglas DC-9-15 G-BFIH (c/n 47048) is at London-Heathrow in June 1978. This aircraft operated with a carrier in Colombia until recently. (John Smith)

Once one of the twin US flag carriers alongside Pan Am, **TWA – Trans World Airlines** was taken over by American Airlines in 2001. Douglas DC-9-15 N1059T (c/n 45740) is pictured at New York-La Guardia in June 1976. This aircraft has been converted to a corporate aircraft, with an executive interior, and is still in operation. (Bob O'Brien)

Pictured at New York-La Guardia in July 1970 is Douglas DC-9-15 N96S (c/n 47206) of **Southern Airways**. This Atlanta, Georgia-based carrier merged in 1979 with North Central to form Republic. This aircraft was sold on, withdrawn and stored in Oklahoma in 1999. (Steve Williams)

The series 30 DC-9 featured a stretch of 15ft (4.57m). Seen at New York-JFK in July 1970 is DC-9-31 N977NE (c/n 47095) of **Northeast Airlines**. This company was merged into Delta in 1972 and the aircraft used by a number of carriers until it was withdrawn from use in 2003. (Ken Fielding)

Now known as US Airways, **Allegheny Airlines** operated a large number of domestic services in the eastern states of the USA. Douglas DC-9-31 N964VJ (c/n 47373) is at New York-La Guardia in June 1976. Following a heavy landing at Elmira, New York in 1992 it was deemed to be beyond economic repair. (Bob O'Brien)

Built as a freighter and showing off its large cargo door is Douglas DC-9-32F I-DIBK (c/n 47355) of Italian flag carrier **Alitalia**. It is pictured at Manchester in April 1974. It was sold by the Italians in 1980 and it can be found to this day still operating in America for parcel carrier USA Jet. (Ian Keast)

Aviaco – Aviacion y Comercio SA was a holiday charter company and a subsidiary of Spanish flag carrier Iberia. It was formed in 1948 and merged into the parent company in September 1999. Pictured at Palma-Majorca in November 1974 is Douglas DC-9-32 EC-CGO (c/n 47640). This aircraft joined the parent airline at the merger and was withdrawn from service in October 2001 and put up for sale. It was broken up at Madrid in November 2002 and the cockpit has gone to Malaga.

JAT – Jugoslovenski Aerotransport was once the national airline for a large country, this was of course Yugoslavia. The bitter civil war of the early 1990s has broken the former country into a number of separate republics. JAT now only represents Serbia and Montenegro, both independent federal units each with its own president. Pictured at Zurich in July 1970 is Douglas DC-9-32 YU-AHO (c/n 47472). This aircraft was sold in America in 1987 and operated until 2003 when it was withdrawn and stored.

North Central Airlines was based at Minneapolis and operated scheduled passenger services around the region. Pictured at New York-La Guardia in June 1976 is Douglas DC-9-32 N942N (c/n 47459). This company merged with Southern to form Republic, which was in turn taken over by Northwest. This aircraft has served with all of these carriers and continues to do so to this day. (Bob O'Brien)

Once one of Yugoslavia's holiday charter operators, Inex Adria Aviopromet have now evolved into Adria Airways of Slovenia. This role as a scheduled passenger carrier follows on from the break-up of the former federation. Douglas DC-9-32 YU-AHJ (c/n 47239) is pictured at Brussels in August 1970. This aircraft can now be found flying for a low-cost airline in the Philippines.

It would have been hard for many people to imagine that a carrier like Swissair could ever fail and disappear from the airports of the world. Douglas DC-9-32 HB-IFK (c/n 45792) is pictured departing Geneva in July 1970. The aircraft was sold to an American airline, retired in 1999 and broken up the following year.

Formed in 1950 **ONA – Overseas National Airways** specialised in charter work for the US military. Pictured on the ramp at Norfolk Naval Air Station, Virginia, on such a charter in May 1972 is Douglas DC-9-32F N938F (c/n 47221). The airline ceased operations in September 1978 and this aircraft was sold to the US Navy who continue to operate it under military markings. (Steve Williams)

Japanese scheduled passenger carrier **TOA Domestic Airlines** evolved into Japan Air System. Pictured at Tokyo-Haneda in May 1977 is Douglas DC-9-41 JA8432 (c/n 47615). The 40 series of the DC-9 was a 74in (1.88m) stretch over the 30 series, bringing the aircraft to an overall length of 125ft 7in (38.25m). This aircraft was sold to American cargo carrier Airborne Express in 1991 and is still in service. (Bob O'Brien)

One of the few multi-nation airlines of the world is **SAS – Scandinavian Airlines System**. It operates for Denmark, Norway and Sweden with aircraft registered in all three countries. Pictured at London-Heathrow in June 1978 is Douglas DC-9-41 OY-KGA (c/n 47115). This aircraft was sold to American passenger carrier Northwest, which continues to operate it.

Showing off a non-standard special livery is **SAS** Douglas DC-9-41 OY-KGS (c/n 47766) at London-Heathrow in September 1979. This aircraft was sold in the USA and placed in storage at Roswell, New Mexico in 2002. (John Smith)

The last version of the true DC-9 before the MD-80 was the 50 series. This 96in (2.44m) stretch brought this model to 133ft 7in (40.7m), a total growth of 29ft 2in (8.84m) over the DC-9-10 series. Pictured at London-Heathrow in June 1978 is Douglas DC-9-51 OE-LDO (c/n 47756) of **Austrian Airlines**, that country's flag carrier. This aircraft, like so many of its type, is still flying Northwest passengers around the USA.

The Boeing 737 has proven to be the best-selling jet airliner the world has yet seen. First flown in April 1967 it is still in production, albeit in a very much more modern version, thirty-eight years later. Pictured at London-Heathrow in June 1978 is 737-130 D-ABET (c/n 19030) of German flag carrier **Lufthansa**. This airline was the launch customer for the type receiving its first in April 1968. The -100 series had a production run of just 30 airframes. The pictured aircraft was sold to a US airline in 1981, being retired and stored in 1998. (John Smith)

The -200 series of the Boeing 737 became the 'default' variant with a stretch of 78in (1.98m) in the fuselage. It was in production into the 1980s before being replaced by the re-engined and further stretched -300 series. Pictured at Orange Country, California in October 1979 is 737-293 N461GB (c/n 19306) of **Air California**. This carrier operated scheduled passenger services in its home state and changed its name to Air Cal in April 1981. This airframe was withdrawn and presented to Phoenix Airport, Arizona where it was used as a fire and rescue training aid. (John Smith)

America's **United Airlines** is one of the biggest passenger carriers in the world. Once just a domestic airline their aircraft can now be seen worldwide. Pictured at San Francisco in October 1979 is Boeing 737-222 N9014U (c/n 19052). This aircraft was withdrawn for spare parts use in 1992 and broken up.

Based in Oslo, Norway, **Mey-Air** was a holiday charter operator. Boeing 737-201 LN-MTC (c/n 20453) is pictured at Palma-Majorca in November 1973. In February of the following year operations were suspended. This aircraft flew with a number of American carriers before it was withdrawn from service in 1999.

British holiday charter carrier **Britannia Airways'** first pure jet was the Boeing 737. Their first one was delivered in July 1968. Pictured at its Luton base in August 1971 is 737-204 G-AWSY (c/n 20236). Following service in America this aircraft was retired from use in the Philippines in 1998. (John Smith)

Southwest Airlines of Dallas, Texas, is the role model for most of the current low-cost, no-frills carriers in the world. They continue to grow, offering low fares and high frequency, yet can still add a sense of fun. They have based their fleet upon the Boeing 737, except for a small number of 727s operated for a short time, and currently fly -300, -500 and -700 series. Pictured in October 1979 at San Antonio, Texas, is 737-2H4 N56SW (c/n 21721). This aircraft was sold to Royal Airlines, later Canada 3000, in Canada and then withdrawn and stored in 2001. (John Smith)

Being formed in 1925 **Western Airlines** could claim to be one of the oldest US carriers. They were taken over by Delta Air Lines in 1987 and merged into its operations. Pictured at San Francisco in October 1979 is Boeing 737-247 N4514W (c/n 19611). This aircraft took up a Russian registration and was withdrawn and stored in Taiwan in 2002.

Wien Air Alaska flew services within America's largest state as well as to the 'lower 48'. Operations were suspended in 1984. Pictured at the Anchorage base in May 1977 is Boeing 737-210C N4902W (c/n 20440). It was last operated in Algeria by Antinea Airlines, which ceased operations in April 2003. (Bob O'Brien)

The first medium-range western passenger-jet was the Sud Aviation SE-210 Caravelle. First flown in May 1955 it entered service with SAS in April 1959 who operated a Copenhagen to Beirut flight. They beat the largest customer, Air France, by a little over a week. They had done this by borrowing one of the prototypes to assist in pilot training. Their own first aircraft was the third production machine. **SAS** Caravelle III OY-KRF (c/n 170) is seen at Manchester in August 1972. This aircraft ended its days in Taiwan where it was withdrawn and stored in October 1979. (Bob O'Brien)

The French flag carrier, **Air France**, was the largest user of the Caravelle with 50 aircraft operated, although not at the same time. They first put the type into operation in May 1959 with a service from Paris to Istanbul. SE-210 Caravelle III F-BHRO (c/n 41) is at Manchester in August 1977. It was retired the following year and later scrapped at Angers-Avrille. (John Smith)

Paris-based, **Air Charter International** was a wholly owned subsidiary of Air France. Its role was to operate inclusive tours and charter flights, its fleet being drawn from the parent company. SE-210 Caravelle III F-BJTJ (c/n 119) is at Paris-Le Bourget in May 1973. This aircraft was sold in Africa, retired in Zaïre and broken up in 1992.

Royal Air Maroc was an early user of the Caravelle. Being a former colonial power, French influence was strong. The first RAM service was Casablanca to Paris in May 1960. SE-210 Caravelle III CN-CCX (c/n 57) is at London-Heathrow in March 1973. This aircraft was withdrawn from service in May 1976 and survives at Casablanca in the Institute of Air Transport. (Steve Williams)

Air Inter was a French scheduled passenger carrier. As well as domestic flights long-haul charters were flown. The company was taken over by Air France in the 1990s and renamed Air Inter Europe. SE-210 Caravelle III F-BNKC (c/n 217) is at Paris-Orly in July 1970. In 1983 it was sold in Africa and retired in Nigeria five years later.

The national carrier of the Grand Duchy of Luxembourg, Luxair, did not start Caravelle services until March 1970. A total of three were operated. SE-210 Caravelle VI-R LX-LGG (c/n 156) is at Palma-Majorca in January 1972. This aircraft was sold in Ecuador in 1978 for spares and broken up. (John Smith)

Madrid-based, **Aviaco** was owned by Iberia and later merged into it. SE-210 Caravelle VI-R EC-ARI (c/n 107) is pictured at Palma-Majorca in November 1973. It was withdrawn at Madrid in 1977 and broken up.

SATA – Societe Anonyme de Transport Aerien was a Swiss holiday charter carrier based in Geneva. Operations were suspended in October 1978. SE-210 Caravelle 10R HB-ICN (c/n 253) is at Liverpool-Speke in June 1970. This airframe can be found preserved in the Turkish Aviation Museum in Istanbul. (Steve Williams)

Based in Palma-Majorca, **TAE – Trabajos Aereos y Enlaces SA** operated a pair of Caravelles. They were obtained from Danish carrier Sterling. SE-210 Caravelle 10B EC-CMS (c/n 238) is at Manchester in September 1979. It was withdrawn from use at Copenhagen in 1991 and survives today as a fire service training aid. (John Smith)

Transeuropa was a Spanish holiday charter operator based at Palma-Majorca. It merged into Aviaco in 1982. Pictured at Palma in November 1973 is SE-210 Caravelle 11R EC-BRX (c/n 261). It was sold in Colombia and damaged beyond repair whilst landing in November 1986.

The first independent airline to operate the Caravelle in Europe was the large German charter carrier **LTU – Luft Transport Unternehmen**. Its first service was in February 1965. Pictured on the ramp at the company's Düsseldorf base in July 1970 is SE-210 Caravelle 10R D-ANYL (c/n 247). It was sold on to a number of European carriers, being withdrawn in 1988 at Bordeaux and then broken up.

National flag carrier **Finnair** first introduced the Caravelle in 1960. They were later replaced by DC-9s. Pictured at London-Heathrow in June 1978 is SE-210 Caravelle 10B3 OH-LSC (c/n 185). This aircraft was later sold to a French company and withdrawn at Perpignan in 1995 and then broken up. (John Smith)

One of the most successful British airliners was the BAC One-Eleven. Designed as a short/medium-haul replacement for the Viscount, it first flew in August 1963. Launch customer was the then newly formed **British United Airways** who operated their first service with the new design in April 1965. Pictured at the company's London-Gatwick base in May 1970 is BAC One-Eleven 510EX G-AWYV (c/n 178). BUA merged with Caledonian to form BCAL (British Caledonian) in 1970 whilst this aircraft was sold on to a number of countries and finally retired at the end of 2001.

The penetration of the American market was a great success for the BAC One-Eleven and large numbers were sold to operators there. BAC One-Eleven 401K N5023 (c/n 063) of **American Airlines** is pictured at New York-La Guardia in July 1970. At this time AA was still a domestic airline and not, as now, one of the world's largest international carriers. This airframe was sold on and, having been retired from service in Guatemala in April 2003, is now derelict. (Steve Williams)

Based at Utica in upstate New York, **Mohawk Airlines** was one of the first American carriers to operate the BAC One-Eleven. In 1972 they were acquired by Allegheny and merged into their network. Pictured at Newark, New Jersey in July 1970 is BAC One-Eleven 204AF N2111J (c/n 029). This aircraft spent most of its working life in the USA and returned to the UK in 1991 to be broken up for spare parts. (Steve Williams)

UK independent scheduled passenger carrier **Cambrian Airways** was formed in 1935. It became a totally-owned part of British Air Services in 1967 and by 1972 it was a regional division of BA and absorbed into the main carrier. BAC One-Eleven 408EF G-AVGP (c/n 114) is pictured, in a mix of BA/Cambrian colours, at Palma, Majorca in November 1974. This aircraft was sold to an operator in South Africa and is currently in store at Johannesburg-Lanseria.

The 1974 merging of BEA and BOAC to form **British Airways** meant a repaint for the BEA fleet in the new colours. BAC One-Eleven 416EK G-AVOF (c/n 131) is at Liverpool-Speke in October 1975. This airframe was sold to Nigeria, like so many of its type, and withdrawn and stored at Benin City in 1997. (Bob O'Brien)

British carrier **Dan-Air** has used the BAC One-Eleven for both scheduled and charter passenger services. Pictured at Palma-Majorca in November 1973 is BAC One-Eleven 414EG G-AZED (c/n 127). This airframe was withdrawn from use at Hurn, UK and then broken up in 2000.

British Caledonian Airways were once the second airline of the UK and flew scheduled passenger services on both long- and short-haul operations. In 1988 they were taken over by British Airways. Pictured at Glasgow in October 1976 is BAC One-Eleven 518FX G-AYOP (c/n 233). This aircraft is currently in store at Maiduguri, Nigeria.

Founded in 1966, **Laker Airways** had at its helm one of the great personalities of British aviation, Mr (later Sir) Freddie Laker. The company operated holiday charter flights and was a pioneer in low-cost transatlantic services. Photographed at Manchester in August 1976 is BAC One-Eleven 310AG G-ATPK (c/n 034). The carrier suspended services in February 1982 and this airframe went on to Nigeria where it was eventually retired from service at the end of 1997. (Bob O'Brien)

Today **Monarch Airlines** operates a fleet of Airbus and Boeing jets to serve both long and short-haul holiday flights. Pictured at Manchester in October 1975 is BAC One-Eleven 517FE G-BCXR (c/n 198). Sold on in 1983, it stayed with UK operators before being withdrawn and broken up in 1992. (Ken Fielding)

At the start of 1970 British holiday charter carrier Autair renamed itself **Court Line**. They stood out from the crowd by having each of their aircraft painted in pastel colours such as pink, orange or turquoise. The cabin crew and the interiors of the aircraft were also colour co-ordinated. Pictured at Manchester in May 1972 is BAC One-Eleven 518FG G-AXMI (c/n 203) in a pink scheme. It is of note that the hostess in the doorway awaiting passengers wears orange and so there is a clash of colours! The company ceased trading in August 1974. This aircraft stayed in the UK and was eventually withdrawn at Southend in November 2000. (Ken Fielding)

Pictured on departure from Palma-Majorca in November 1973 is BAC One-Eleven 518FG G-AXMK (c/n 205) of **Court Line**. This aircraft is in the orange scheme. It operated for a number of subsequent airlines before being withdrawn at Southend in November 1992 and then broken up.

German holiday charter operator **Bavaria Flug** bought new BAC One-Elevens from the manufacturer. They operated from such sites as Munich to the holiday resorts of Spain. The carrier merged with Germanair in 1977 and the new company was quickly taken over by Hapag-Lloyd. BAC One-Eleven 414 D-AILY (c/n 163) is pictured on a wet Cologne ramp in July 1970. This aircraft was converted to an executive configuration and still operates in this form today.

Pictured on the ramp at the company's Bahrain base in November 1976 is BAC One-Eleven 432FD A4O-BU (c/n 157) of **Gulf Air**. This aircraft later returned to the UK and then to Nigeria. It was withdrawn and stored at Benin City at the end of 1997. (Bob O'Brien)

Pictured at London-Gatwick in April 1970 is BAC One-Eleven 510EX G-AWYS (c/n 175) in the livery of **Swissair**. This carrier leased a BUA example for a six-month period. The aircraft was sold on and went to Nigeria where it was retired and stored in 2001. (Ken Fielding)

The British colony of the Cayman Islands is a renowned tax haven in the Caribbean. **Cayman Airways** operate from the capital Georgetown on Grand Cayman Island. The airline's current fleet is five Boeing 737s. Pictured at Miami in April 1977 is BAC One-Eleven 531FS TI-LRJ (c/n 244). This aircraft was on lease from LACSA of Costa Rica. It returned to serve in the UK and was retired at Southend in 1992, being broken up six years later. (Bob O'Brien)

Air Pacific is the current flag carrier for the Republic of Fiji. They currently have an all-Boeing fleet and operate services as far as the USA. Pictured at Brisbane, Australia in December 1979 is BAC One-Eleven 479FU DQ-FBQ (c/n 245). This aircraft joined the British military and is now a radar trials testbed with FRA Aviation at Bournemouth-Hurn. (Bob O'Brien)

Whilst producing the most successful of the turboprop 'DC-3 replacements' Fokker of Holland designed and built the F.28 Fellowship, powered by a pair of Rolls-Royce Spey jets of 9,750 lb thrust. It was aimed at the short-haul market and its original 65-seat capacity well suited this. Launch customer was German holiday charter carrier **LTU – Luft Transport Unternehmen**. Pictured at Frankfurt in July 1970 is D-ABAX (c/n 11006). This airframe is currently serving with Aero Continente in Lima, Peru.

Pictured at London-Gatwick in May 1970 is Fokker F.28 Fellowship 1000 I-TIDE (c/n 11015) of Rome-based **Itavia (Societa Aerolinee)**. The airline ceased services in December 1980 and this aircraft was destroyed in a landing crash at Turin in January 1974. (Ken Fielding)

Formed in 1927, the Spanish flag carrier **Iberia** is based in Madrid and flies services worldwide. They bought three F.28s that were delivered in 1970, but only operated them for four years before selling them. F.28 Fellowship 1000 EC-BVC (c/n 11023) is in the manufacturer's flight sheds at Amsterdam-Schiphol in July 1970. This aircraft was damaged beyond economic repair following a landing accident at Bilbao in December 1972.

Pictured at Palma-Majorca in January 1972 is Fokker F.28 Fellowship 1000 D-AHLA (c/n 11027) of German holiday charter carrier **Aviaction**. They were based in the port city of Hamburg and commenced services in March 1971. Operations ceased in October 1973. This aircraft operated for a number of airlines and is currently in store at Bamako in Africa. (John Smith)

Norwegian passenger carrier **Braathens – SAFE** (South American and Far East) was the airline arm of a shipping company. It is now part of the SAS group of companies. F.28 Fellowship 1000 LN-SUO (c/n 11013) is on the manufacturer's ramp at Amsterdam-Schiphol in July 1970. This aircraft later operated in France and was withdrawn from use at Dinard in October 1993.

The original TAT was **Touraine Air Transport**. In 1984 it was renamed Transport Aérien Transregional. The French scheduled passenger carrier flew domestic and regional European services. F.28 Fellowship 1000 F-GBBS (c/n 11050) is at London-Heathrow in September 1979. The airline merged with Air Liberté in October 1997. This aircraft was sold in Canada and later withdrawn and stored in May 2002. (John Smith)

Formed by a merger in 1963, VFW (Vereinigte Flugtechnische Werke) designed and built one of the least successful airliners of the 1970s. The most unconventional feature was the placement of the engines: a pair of RR-SNECMA M45 turbofans of 7,480 lb thrust being mounted on pylons on top of the wings. **VFW 614** D-BABC (c/n MG-03) is pictured at the Farnborough Air Show in September 1974 in the manufacturer's house colours. A total of 19 airframes were built and flown. In a 44-seat configuration it served with a handful of airlines. The last operator was the German Luftwaffe who used them in a VIP role. The pictured aircraft was never put into commercial service, it was retired in 1976 and broken up in 1981.

The Vickers VC-10 was an elegant-looking airliner designed for BOAC's routes in Africa and the Far East where good 'hot and high' performance was required. It found much passenger favour on the North Atlantic routes. Pictured at London-Heathrow in June 1978 is VC-10 9G-ABO (c/n 823) of **Ghana Airways**. This aircraft was bought new in 1965, withdrawn at the end of 1980 and then broken up in Scotland. (John Smith)

Bahrain-based **Gulf Air** bought their VC-10s from BOAC. Pictured on the Bahrain ramp in May 1977 is A4O-VL (c/n 814). This aircraft later joined the RAF and was converted to an in-flight refuelling tanker. It was withdrawn and scrapped at St Athan in Wales during 2000. (Bob O'Brien)

Bought new in September 1964, **British Caledonian** operated this VC-10 until 1974. G-ASIW (c/n 819) is pictured landing at London-Gatwick in January 1974. It was sold on to Air Malawi, retired and broken up in 1981. (John Smith)

The Vickers Super VC-10 was a 13ft (3.96m) stretch of the fuselage of the VC-10 giving extra range and seating capacity. G-ASGK (c/n 861) of **British Airways** is seen at Prestwick in October 1976. It joined the RAF in 1981 but was not converted to a tanker role and broken up for spares at Abingdon.

Pictured at Manchester in June 1970 is Super VC-10 G-ASGF (c/n 856) in the classic livery of **BOAC**. This aircraft also joined the RAF in 1981 and was broken up for spares the following year. The nose and cockpit section was retained and used as a simulator for training flight crews. (Ken Fielding)

Based in Nairobi, **East African Airways** was set up in 1946 to cover the territories of Kenya, Tanganyika, Uganda and Zanzibar. Following independence all these countries formed their own national airlines. Pictured at London-Heathrow in August 1970 is Vickers Super VC-10 5X-UVA (c/n 881). This aircraft was burnt out following an aborted take-off at Addis Ababa in April 1972. (Steve Williams)

First flown in January 1962, the de Havilland Trident was a short- to medium-range airliner, powered by three Rolls-Royce Spey 505 jets of 9,850 lb thrust. The aircraft had been tailored to the needs of launch customer BEA. It was this factor that hampered sales to other carriers. HS.121 Trident 1C G-ARPP (c/n 2117) of **British Airways** is seen at Glasgow in October 1976 operating the service to London. This aircraft was withdrawn from use at this location in February 1983 and used by the fire service as a training aid.

To boost sales, de Havilland (Hawker Siddeley) produced the Trident 1E. This version had an increased wingspan, greater fuel capacity, and Spey 511 engines with 11,400 lb of thrust. Passenger load increased from 103 to 115 and for the Trident 1E-140 to 139 in a high-density configuration. HS.121 Trident 1E-140 G-AVYE (c/n 2139) is at Palma-Majorca in November 1973 in the final livery of **BEA**. The following year the company merged with BOAC to form British Airways. This airframe was donated to the Science Museum and displayed as part of their collection at Wroughton. It was later replaced by another Trident, taken to Hatfield and used as a fire trial aircraft.

In 1970 UK scheduled passenger carrier BKS changed their name to **Northeast**. This was to reflect the geographic region of England it largely served. Three years later, via their parent company they became part of BA. Pictured in a hybrid scheme at Palma, Majorca in November 1973 is Hawker Siddeley HS.121 Trident 1E -140 G-AVYB (c/n 2136). This aircraft was withdrawn from use at London-Heathrow in 1980 and broken up the following year. The fuselage was moved to Hereford for use as a training aid by the Special Air Service regiment of the British Army and eventually scrapped.

The Trident 2E was first flown in July 1967; its increased wing span, fuel capacity and engine power enabled it to operate UK to the Middle East routes. **Cyprus Airways** was a customer for this variant. HS.121 Trident 2E 5B-DAB (c/n 2155) is at Manchester in July 1973. This aircraft was destroyed at Nicosia Airport during a bombing raid by the Turkish Air Force in July 1974. This action led to the partition of the island that continues to this day. (Ken Fielding)

The final variant of the Trident was the 3B. This had a stretched fuselage and an extra engine in the base of the fin. This Rolls-Royce RB162 produced 5,250 lb of thrust and was used for take-offs from short runways or with high operating weights. Pictured at Palma-Majorca in November 1973 is Trident 3B G-AWYZ (c/n 2301) in the hybrid colours of the newly formed **British Airways**. This airframe, the first of the type, was withdrawn from service at Heathrow in 1983 and broken up the following year.

UK independent **Dan-Air** had a huge fleet of Comets; operating over forty 4, 4B and 4C versions, although not all at once. Some of the airframes were bought just for spares reclamation. Pictured on a holiday charter, de Havilland DH.106 Comet 4 G-APYC (c/n 6437) retracts its undercarriage whilst climbing out of Palma, Majorca in November 1973. This aircraft was sold to the Ministry of Defence in December 1978 and used for assault training by the Army at Kemble. It was sold for scrap at the end of 1982.

Pictured at Manchester in January 1975 is **Dan-Air** DH.106 Comet 4B G-APMD (c/n 6435). The '4B' was the short- to medium-range variant of the type. This aircraft was retired to the company base at Lasham the same month and broken up the following year. (Ian Keast)

The de Havilland Comet will forever be remembered as the first pure jet airliner to enter service. This was in May 1952 when BOAC operated a London to South Africa service. The early accidents, caused by metal fatigue, led to the end of the Comet 1 but from this led to the Comet 4. The final variant was the '4C' with both long range and high capacity (for its time). Pictured at Lasham in July 1975 is DH.106 Comet 4C ST-AAX (c/n 6463) in the livery of **Sudan Airways**. The aircraft had just been delivered to UK carrier Dan-Air who operated it until November 1979 when it was withdrawn from use at Lasham and then broken up the following year. This aircraft was the last civil Comet to operate a fare-paying passenger service. (John Smith)

The Boeing 727 was the world's best-selling airliner until it lost that crown to its baby brother, the 737, racking up a sales total of 1832 aircraft. 727-30 D-ABIR (c/n 18933) of German holiday charter carrier **Condor** is pictured on the ramp at Stuttgart in July 1970. This aircraft was sold in the USA, converted to an executive interior and is currently based at Kinshasa, Zaïre.

Until the re-unification of Germany in the 1990s, German carriers were not allowed to fly to Berlin. This followed the Four Powers Agreement at the end of World War Two that the divided city could only be served by British, French or American airlines. Lufthansa, when it was reformed in 1954, was not allowed into Berlin. One of the companies operating these services was the American flag-carrier **Pan American**. Boeing 727-21 N329PA (c/n 19038) is pictured on the runway at London-Heathrow in June 1978. The airline ceased operations in December 1991 following mounting losses. This aircraft was converted to a freighter in 1985 and operated by Emery Worldwide until withdrawn and stored at Goodyear, AZ in 2001.

American Airlines is today one of the world's largest carriers having been in the 1960s and 1970s largely a domestic airline. They were one of the major operators of the three-engined Boeing. 727-23 N1998 (c/n 19129) is pictured at San Francisco in October 1979. This aircraft was sold in Africa and was withdrawn and stored at St Pietersburg, South Africa, at the end of 2000. (John Smith)

Canadian charter carrier Wardair operated passenger services across the Atlantic with 727s. 727-11 CF-FUN (c/n 19242) is pictured at Manchester in June 1970. The airline was taken over by Canadian Airlines in January 1990 and this aircraft was sold in South America. It was retired at Bogota, Colombia and was being stripped for spares at the end of 1997. (Ken Fielding)

From its central location for operations to either side of the Atlantic, **Icelandair** has long connected the United Kingdom with Reykjavik. Pictured at London-Heathrow in September 1979 is Boeing 727-185C TF-FLG (c/n 19826). Sold on, this airframe has been converted to a 'Quiet Freighter' and has been re-engined with Rolls-Royce Tay jets. It serves today with UPS, one of the large American parcel delivery companies. (John Smith)

Japan Air Lines operates two divisions today. One is international services and the other domestic, the latter with high-density seating aircraft. Pictured at Tokoyo-Haneda in May 1977 is Boeing 727-46 JA8327 (c/n 20078). Sold on, this aircraft was converted to a freighter and crashed in Angola in January 2001. (Bob O'Brien)

Based in Minneapolis, Northwest Airlines is today one of the biggest American carriers with services worldwide. They have a large number of services to Japan and this explains their previous name, **Northwest Orient Airlines**. 727-251 N253US (c/n 19972) is at San Francisco in October 1979. The -200 series of the 727 was a fuselage stretch of two 10ft (3.05m) sections, one ahead and the other behind the wing. Over 1200 aircraft were built. This airframe was sold in Nigeria and then stored following the demise of its operator.

American carrier **Northeast Airlines** was taken over by Delta Air Lines in 1972. Pictured at New York-JFK in July 1970 is Boeing 727-295 N1646 (c/n 20140). It was withdrawn from service in Texas in 1990 and then broken up. (Ken Fielding)

Based at New York-JFK, **Trans Caribbean** was a scheduled passenger carrier serving such locations as the US Virgin Islands and Puerto Rico. They were taken over by American Airlines in May 1971. Photographed at JFK in July 1970 is Boeing 727-2A7 N8790R (c/n 20240). This aeroplane crashed whilst landing at St Thomas, US Virgin Islands, in December of that year. (Ken Fielding)

Like many European airlines, Italian flag-carrier **Alitalia** operated 727s until they were replaced by newer Airbus designs. Pictured at London-Heathrow in June 1978 is 727-243 I-DIRJ (c/n 21270). This aircraft was sold in Canada where it still operates with Kelowna Flightcraft.

JAT – Jugoslovenski Aerotransport, as stated earlier, now only represents a small fraction of that divided nation. 727-2H9 YU-AKF (c/n 21038) is at London-Heathrow in June 1978. Bought new in 1975 by the carrier, they still own it. It is, however, in store at its Belgrade base.

Once just a domestic carrier, Japan's **All Nippon Airways** can now be found operating overseas. Pictured at its Tokyo-Haneda base in May 1977 is 727-281 JA8331 (c/n 20469). It was sold to Korea and damaged beyond repair following a belly landing at Taegu in August 1991. (Bob O'Brien)

Based in San Diego, California, **PSA – Pacific Southwest Airlines** flew passengers up and down the Pacific coast and to nearby western states. They were merged into US Air in 1988. Pictured at San Francisco in October 1979 is 727-214 N545PS (c/n 20169). This aircraft was sold on and ended its days in Buenos Aires, Argentina, where it was broken up in 2000.

Iberia, the Spanish flag carrier, operated the 727 from 1972 through to 2000. Pictured at Palma-Majorca in November 1973 is 727-256 EC-CBF (c/n 20600). The airline had this airframe from new in March 1973 and retired it in 2000. It now flies for a Jordanian company, but is registered in Swaziland.

United Airlines are today the world's biggest airline with extensive international and domestic routes. Pictured at New York-La Guardia in June 1976 is Boeing 727-222 N7639U (c/n 19912). It shows an old, but still smart, livery. Sold on, this aircraft was converted to a freighter and was operated as a parcel carrier in the USA by Emery Worldwide until 2004. (Bob O'Brien)

Delta Air Lines of Atlanta, Georgia, is one of the large American 'legacy' carriers, with services both domestic and international. Pictured at San Francisco in October 1979 is 727-295 N1640 (c/n 19445). Sold on to other US airlines, it was eventually retired and broken up in Texas during 1993.

Seen at London-Heathrow in June 1978 is **Libyan Arab Airlines** Boeing 727-2L5 5A-DID (c/n 21229). The airline was absent from the airports of Europe for some years, due to the country's involvement with terrorist activities. All that ended in 2004 when limited services were resumed. The aircraft was delivered new in July 1976 and is still owned by the carrier, albeit in a stored condition at Tripoli following years of sanctions. (John Smith)

Showing off the classic old livery of **Air France** is Boeing 727-228 F-BPJI (c/n 19865). It is seen at Paris-Charles de Gaulle in May 1977. Sold on to Key Airlines it was withdrawn and broken up at Oklahoma City in 1993.

With the current 'modern' livery is **Air France** Boeing 727-228 F-BPJO (c/n 20410). It is pictured at Paris-Charles de Gaulle in May 1977. Sold on to an American carrier it was withdrawn and broken up at Oklahoma City in 1992.

Like Boeing and Douglas, Convair designed and built a four-engined jet airliner, the Convair 880. Unlike the other two aircraft, it did not sell in any great numbers and was a financial disaster for the company. The aircraft were, however, elegant and faster than their rivals. With a narrower fuselage they only had five-across seating thus costing more per seat-mile than the 707 or DC-8. Pictured at Pittsburgh in August 1970 is Convair 880 N806TW (c/n 22-00-8) of **Trans World Airways**. This aircraft was retired in August 1978 and, like so many of its type, stored at Mojave, California, before being broken up in 2000. (Steve Williams)

The Convair 880 was the first jet airliner operated by **LANICA** of Nicaragua. They started operations with the new type in July 1972 and flew their last service in June 1977. During that time six aircraft were operated but not together. Photographed at Miami in April 1976 is Convair 880-22-1 AN-BIA (c/n 22-00-39). It was sold on, retired and broken up in 1984. (Bob O'Brien)

After airline service in the Far East, Convair 880-22M N88CH (c/n 22-7-6-58) was converted to an executive interior in 1976. Operated by the **Hirschmann Corporation**, it was used for executive charters. It is pictured at Paris-Le Bourget in June 1977. This airframe had an unusual end. It was sold to a carrier in South Africa who did not put it into service. It was then sold to a private individual who transported the fuselage to Bonza Bay in East London, South Africa where it is used as a holiday home.

Following the low sales of the 880 (just sixty-five), Convair produced the 990. It had a 10ft (3.05m) fuselage stretch, new engines, General Electric CJ-805 turbofans of 16,100 lb thrust each and capacity for 121 passengers. It was to be the fastest airliner until the arrival of the SSTs. Pictured at Zurich in June 1973 is Convair 990-30A-6 HB-ICB of **Swissair**. (c/n 30-10-11). It was retired and broken up at Hamburg in April 1975. (John Smith)

APSA – Aerolineas Peruanas SA was based in the capital Lima. They operated three 990s but ceased operations in May 1971. Pictured in store at Marana, Arizona in October 1979 is Convair 990-30A-6 N990AC (c/n 30-10-5). The fate of this aircraft was to remain stored at this location and it is currently without any wings.

Photographed at Palma-Majorca in November 1973 is Convair 990-30A N5623 (c/n 30-10-20) of **Modern Air**. This carrier was a non-scheduled American airline who operated holiday charter flights from Berlin. They suspended all services in October 1976. The aircraft was sold on and retired to Marana, Arizona in December 1984, where it was broken up two years later.

Palma-based Spanish holiday charter carrier **Spantax** was one of the largest operators of the 990 as well as being the last. They remained in service until March 1987. Pictured at Palma in January 1972 is Convair 990-30A-5 EC-BTE (c/n 30-10-21). This aircraft was withdrawn from service in October 1981 and scrapped in 1991. (Steve Williams)

Although it was outsold by the Boeing 707 by a large margin, the Douglas DC-8 has carried on and on to this date by virtue of its excellent and flexible design. The first DC-8 was flown, in May 1958, from the company's Long Beach plant. It had the same basic layout as the 707 and the Convair 880. Pan American and United were the launch customers. **Air Spain** was a Spanish holiday charter carrier, which commenced operations with Bristol Britannias in March 1967. It replaced them with DC-8s in 1973 and ceased services at the start of 1975. Pictured climbing out of Palma-Majorca in November 1973 is DC-8-21 EC-CDA (c/n 45429). Eagle-eyed readers will spot that this is the same airframe as the Eastern Airlines aircraft illustrated on the opposite page. It was sold on to a number of operators and retired in Holland in 1981, being broken up three years later.

Pictured at New York-JFK in July 1970 is DC-8-21 N8608 (c/n 45429) in the colours of Miami-based **Eastern Airlines**. The carrier did not survive the rigours of deregulation and suspended services at the start of 1991. This aircraft was sold to Spanish airline Air Spain. (Ken Fielding)

When the Belgian Congo became independent Zaïre in 1961, a national airline was formed to carry the flag. **Air Zaïre** continued operations until June 1995. Pictured at Zurich in June 1973 is Douglas DC-8-32 9Q-CLE (c/n 45266). This aircraft was withdrawn the following year and broken up at its Kinshasa base. (John Smith)

TAE – Trabajos Aeroeos y Enlaces was a Spanish holiday charter carrier based on the island of Majorca. Pictured at its Palma base in November 1974 is Douglas DC-8-32 EC-CDC (c/n 45567). The airline suspended services in 1981 and this airframe was retired at Palma in 1982 and subsequently broken up.

During its life the DC-8 has been fitted with several different engines. The -40 series were powered by four Rolls-Royce Conway jets with an output of 17,500 lb thrust each. Pictured at Manchester in August 1976 is Douglas DC-8-43 C-FCPJ (c/n 45661) of **CP Air**, formerly Canadian Pacific Airlines. The carrier merged with Pacific Western in April 1987 to form Canadian Airlines. This aeroplane was sold to a Colombian operator at the end of 1981, which broke it up for spare parts. (Bob O'Brien)

Spanish national carrier **Iberia** operated DC-8s on both long-haul and domestic services. DC-8-52 EC-ARB (c/n 45618) is pictured at Palma-Majorca in November 1973. The -50 series was a long-range version powered by Pratt & Whitney JT3D turbofans with 17,000 lb of thrust each. Sold on in 1977, it had a number of operators before being used for spare parts at Detroit-Willow Run in 1992.

Pictured at Palma-Majorca in November 1974 is Douglas DC-8-52 EC-ATP (c/n 45658) of Spanish holiday charter carrier **Aviaco**. This aircraft joined the Spanish Air Force and was then sold on. After further charter work with Canadian operator Holidair the aircraft reverted to executive configuration as VR-BIA. It was retired at Lasham in 1995 and broken up two years later.

Showing off the carrier's classic livery is Douglas DC-8-53 JA8012 (c/n 45680) of **Japan Air Lines**. It is pictured at New York-JFK in July 1970. This aircraft crashed on approach to Delhi, India in June 1972. (Ken Fielding)

Japan Asia Airways was formed in August 1975 to operate services from Tokyo to Taipei (Republic of China). This was because JAL had been granted rights to serve Beijing (People's Republic of China) and the communist authorities would not allow any carrier to serve both locations. JAA is a wholly-owned subsidiary of JAL. Pictured at Tokyo-Haneda in May 1977 is Douglas DC-8-53 JA8007 (c/n 45647). This aircraft was sold to Overseas National as N903R in 1981, then retired to Wilmington, Ohio and broken up in 1986. (Bob O'Brien)

In the -60 series Douglas was able to stretch the fuselage of the DC-8 so it could carry a maximum of 259 passengers (the original model could only carry 176). 20ft (6.10m) was added forward of the wing and 16ft 8in (5.1m) aft. Pictured at Prestwick in October 1976 is DC-8-61 CF-TJW (c/n 45893) of **Air Canada**. This aircraft was sold on in 1986, converted to a freighter three years later, and then retired and broken up at Wilmington, Ohio in 2001.

Spanish carrier **Spantax** used the stretched DC-8s for high-density passenger traffic. Douglas DC-8-61 EC-CCG (c/n 45898) is pictured at Palma-Majorca in November 1974. This airframe is still in service to this day with UPS as a parcel freighter in America, having been re-engined in 1985 with CFM-56s to create a DC-8-71CF.

Pictured at San Francisco in October 1979 is Douglas DC-8-61 N8076U (c/n 45941) of **United Airlines**. Sold on and converted to a -71 series freighter with the new CFM-56 engines, it was withdrawn and stored at Roswell, New Mexico in 2001.

The -62 series DC-8 was a long-range variant. The -50 series fuselage was extended by 3ft 4in (1m) both forward and aft of the wing, while wingspan was expanded by 6ft (1.8m). Pictured at New York-JFK in July 1970 is Douglas DC-8-62CF OH-LFT (c/n 46013) of **Finnair**. Sold on in 1981, it joined the French Air Force where it served until very recently. (Ken Fielding)

Once the largest independent airline in France, **UTA – Union de Transports Aériens** was taken over by Air France in 1992. Pictured at Paris-Le Bourget in July 1970 is DC-8-62 F-BNLE (c/n 45917). This aircraft was sold in 1984, converted to a freighter for Airborne Express and retired at Wilmington, Ohio in 2000.

The DC-8-63 was the logical step of matching the long fuselage of the -61 with the wings of the -62. Douglas DC-8-63 YV-125C (c/n 46042) of **VIASA (Venezolina Internacional de Aviación)** is at London-Heathrow in July 1976. The carrier was the government-owned flag carrier of Venezuela. Following mounting losses it was closed down in January 1997. This aircraft was sold in 1986, converted to a freighter in 1988 and is still active with Arrow Air in the USA. (John Smith)

Trans International Airlines was an American passenger and cargo charter operator. Douglas DC-8-63 N797FT (c/n 46140) is pictured at Paris-Le Bourget in May 1973. The carrier was renamed Transamerica in 1979 and this aircraft was converted to a -73CF series in which guise it still operates with the American parcel company UPS.

SAS – Scandinavian Airlines System is the carrier for Sweden, Norway and Denmark. Douglas DC-8-63 LN-MOY (c/n 46054) is photographed at New York-JFK in July 1970. This aircraft was sold on in 1974, converted to a freight role in 1989 and is currently the sole aircraft of a Mexican cargo airline. (Ken Fielding)

Founded in 1945 as an all-cargo airline, **Flying Tigers** was merged into the Federal Express empire in 1989. Douglas DC-8-63CF N796FT (c/n 46104) is at Los Angeles-LAX in October 1979. Sold on in 1984, it was stored in New Mexico in 2001 and then sold in 2004 to a Brazilian cargo airline where it currently serves.

Founded in 1948 as a charter carrier, **World Airways** flies a mix of passenger and freight services. Douglas DC-8-63CF N802WA (c/n 46146) is seen at London-Gatwick in August 1973. This aircraft crashed in Alaska the following month. (John Smith)

Saudia, later renamed Saudi Arabian Airlines, was the government-owned flag carrier for that nation. Douglas DC-8-63CF N8632 (c/n 45966) is pictured at London-Heathrow in June 1978. This aircraft was converted to a -73CF series for UPS and still currently serves with them. (John Smith)

Based in Tennessee, Capitol Airways was an American charter carrier. Douglas DC-8-63 N4908C (c/n 45968) is pictured on a trooping charter for the US military at Frankfurt in July 1970. The airline suspended services in November 1984. This aircraft, like so many, was converted for cargo and re-engined with CFM-56s to become a -73F. It still operates for American parcel company UPS.

There can be little doubt that the Boeing 707 was the most commercially successful aircraft of its day. With its swept wings and four Pratt & Whitney JT3 turbojets mounted in pods under them, it set a design standard that was often copied. Pictured at Stansted in May 1979 is 707-123B N7521A (c/n 17648) of **Aero America**. The -100 series of the type was both longer, by 10ft (3.05m), and wider than the prototype. Aero America was a carrier who flew charters and sub-leased aircraft to travel clubs. They suspended operations in the following November. This aircraft was withdrawn from service in 1982 at Marana, Arizona and broken up in 1987.

Australia's flag carrier Qantas had a special 'short-body' version of the 707 built for them. The base line -100 was reduced by 10ft (3.05m) to lower the weight of the aircraft and allow a full payload to be carried. They were operated from 1959 to 1967 when they were sold on. Photographed at London-Gatwick in August 1973 is Boeing 707-138B CF-PWV (c/n 17696) of Vancouver-based **Pacific Western Airlines**. The company merged with CP Air to form Canadian Airlines in 1987. This aircraft was converted to an executive aircraft for the Government of Saudi Arabia and then stored in the UK from 1999. Early in 2005 Qantas were surveying the airframe with a view to returning it to Australia as a flying 'heritage' aircraft. (John Smith)

As with all successful designs the 707 came in a number of forms. The -300 was the intercontinental version for non-stop transatlantic operations. Pan American was the launch customer with an order placed in 1955. Pictured at London-Gatwick in September 1973 is 707-321 G-AZWA (c/n 17605) of UK-based holiday charter operator **Donaldson International Airways**. Formed in 1964 they operated until August 1974. This aircraft was sold on and was written off following a landing accident at Bogota, Colombia in December 1980. (John Smith)

Based in the capital Nassau, **Bahamas World Airways** operated charters. Pictured at Paris-Le Bourget in May 1973 is 707-138B VP-BDE (c/n 17700). The carrier ceased operations in 1978 and this aircraft followed the fate of many 707s. It was purchased by the US Air Force and flown to Davis-Monthan Air Force Base at Tucson, Arizona, where it was used for spare parts for their fleet of KC-135 tankers, being eventually broken up in 1993.

Phoenix Airlines of Basel, Switzerland commenced operations in the spring of 1971 and terminated them in 1974. Pictured at Zurich in June 1973 is Boeing 707-131 HB-IEG (c/n 17671). Sold on the aircraft was destroyed, with heavy loss of life, in a crash in Bolivia in October 1976. (John Smith)

The -400 series of the 707 was a -300 fitted with Rolls-Royce Conway jets. The launch customer was BOAC. Pictured at Palma-Majorca in January 1972 is Boeing 707-436 G-APFK (c/n 17712) of **BEA Airtours**. This carrier was formed in 1969 to operate holiday charter flights. With the BEA/BOAC merger in 1974 they became British Airtours. This aircraft was destroyed by fire following a take-off crash at Prestwick during a crew training flight in March 1977. (John Smith)

In 1955 **Air France** became the first non-US carrier to order the 707. Operations commenced in February 1960 and they flew the type into the 1980s. Showing a classic livery at Paris-Charles de Gaulle in May 1977 is Boeing 707-328B F-BHSS (c/n 18246). This aircraft was sold to the Israeli Air Force the following year and in 1995 it moved to Elifelet for conversion to a restaurant.

Transasian Airlines of Luton, UK, were the operating division of leasing company Templewood Aviation. They were renamed Air Transcontinental in 1979 and suspended all services the following year. Boeing 707-321B N762TB (c/n 18337) is at Luton in May 1979. The aircraft served with a number of subsequent operators and was retired for spares use at Marana, Arizona in 1984.

Although **BOAC** were the first airline across the Atlantic Ocean with jets, they operated Comets from October 1958, the type lacked the range of the 707 and so the carrier placed an order in 1956 for fifteen Rolls-Royce Conway-powered aircraft. Boeing 707-465 G-ARWD (c/n 18372) is at Manchester in June 1970. This aircraft was sold on, retired in 1981 and broken up at Kingman, Arizona five years later. (Ken Fielding)

Pictured at Nairobi in March 1977 Boeing 707-321C G-BEAF (c/n 18591) is in the joint livery of its owner Dan-Air and **IAS (International Aviation Services)** to whom it was leased. IAS was renamed British Cargo Airlines in 1979 following a merger with Transmeridian Air Cargo. This airframe was sold in Argentina in 1978 and retired and broken up at the end of 1990. (Bob O'Brien)

TMA – Trans Mediterranean Airways was formed in 1953 as a charter airline carrying freight only. They still operate to this day from their Beirut, Lebanon, base. Pictured at London-Heathrow in June 1978 is Boeing 707-327C N7095 (c/n 19104). This aircraft is still owned by the company albeit in a stored condition at Beirut.

SABENA, the acronym for Société Anonyme Belge d'Exploitations de la Navigation Aérienne, was the Belgian flag carrier with a history dating back to 1923. It ordered the 707 at the same time as Air France and introduced the type to service in January 1960, with flights to New York. In November 2001 the company ceased all operations. Pictured at London-Heathrow in September 1978 is Boeing 707-329C OO-SJJ (c/n 19162). This aircraft was sold in Africa and damaged beyond repair following a heavy landing at Goma, Zaïre in March 1990. (John Smith)

Pan American Airways are perhaps the best known of all the 707 operators. They were the launch customer and over the years purchased 126 new 707s. The first service was in October 1958 with flights from New York to Paris. Following mounting losses the company suspended operations in December 1991. Pictured at Nairobi in March 1977 is Boeing 707-321C N448PA (c/n 19270) configured as a freighter. Sold on, it served in many parts of the world before being retired in Nigeria during 1999 and then broken up. (Bob O'Brien)

British Caledonian Airways was once a major UK-based scheduled and charter passenger carrier. Pictured at Nairobi in March 1977 is Boeing 707-338C G-BCAL (c/n 19297). At the end of 1987 the company was taken over by British Airways. This aircraft was sold in South America, retired in 1988 at Miami, and then broken up. (Bob O'Brien)

Once government-owned, **Korean Air Lines** was privatised in 1969. It is today the largest carrier in that country. Pictured at Bahrain in May 1977 is Boeing 707-373C N370WA (c/n 19442) operating as a freighter. This airframe had a new lease of life when purchased by Northrop-Grumman and converted to an E-8C J-STARS (Joint Surveillance Target Attack Radar System) aircraft for the US Air Force. (Bob O'Brien)

Pictured at Prestwick in October 1976 is Boeing 707-365C G-ATZD (c/n 19590) of **British Airways**. This aircraft has since joined the Argentine Air Force where it serves to this day.

The best known airline in Australia is **Qantas**, once Queensland and Northern Territory Aerial Services. Pictured at Manchester in February 1974 is Boeing 707-338C VH-EAB (c/n 19622). This aircraft has also had a new lease of life, being converted to an E-8C J-STARS for the USAF. (Ken Fielding)

Ontario Worldair was a short-lived Canadian holiday charter airline. Operations commenced at the start of December 1978 and ceased in January 1981. Pictured at Manchester in May 1979 is Boeing 707-338C C-GRYN (c/n 19623). This aircraft joined the Royal Australian Air Force where it still serves. (John Smith)

Kenya Airways is the flag carrier for that country, formed in 1977 following the break up of East African Airways. Boeing 707-351B 5Y-BBJ (c/n 19633) is at London-Heathrow in June 1978. It was retired in 1991 and sold two years later to the government of Botswana. It is still in use with their police force as a ground training aid. (John Smith)

VARIG (Viacao Aerea Rio-Grandense), like a number of carriers in South America, has a long history, dating back to 1927. From their base at Rio de Janeiro, Brazil, they operate worldwide. Pictured at Los Angeles-LAX in October 1976 is Boeing 707-345C PP-VJX (c/n 19842). This aircraft joined the Brazilian Air Force in 1986 and still serves. (Steve Williams)

The Greek national airline is Olympic Airways. They ordered 707s in April 1965 in order to operate a service to New York, this commenced in June of the following year. Pictured at London-Heathrow in June 1978 is Boeing 707-384B SX-DBF (c/n 20036). Its fate was to join the stored aircraft at Davis-Monthan AFB and donate its engines to the USAF KC-135 fleet.

Wardair of Edmonton, Canada, flew international passenger charters. April 1968 saw the delivery of their first 707. The airline was absorbed into Canadian Airlines at the start of 1990. Pictured at Manchester in September 1977 is Boeing 707-396C CF-ZYP (c/n 20043). This aircraft was sold on and in 1981 was seized by the US Customs Service following an attempt to fly arms to South Africa. It was retained by the US authorities, transferred to the USAF in 1985, and converted to an E-8 J-STARS in 2000. (Bob O'Brien)

TWA – Trans World Airways first operated 707s in March 1959 on the New York to San Francisco route. They also operated the shortest sector for the type, a ten-mile trip across the bay from San Francisco to Oakland. Boeing 707-331B N8729 (c/n 20058) is seen at London-Gatwick in August 1973. The airline was taken over by American Airlines in 2001 and this aircraft joined the stored fleet at Davis-Monthan AFB donating spare parts to KC-135s before being broken up. (John Smith)

Formed in 1954 and nationalised in 1962, **Kuwait Airways** first operated 707s in November 1968. Pictured at London-Heathrow in June 1978 is Boeing 707-369C 9K-ACL (c/n 20086). This aircraft was sold to Sudan Airways in 1984 who later retired it and broke it up for spare parts at Khartoum.

Today one of the world's largest carriers, **American Airlines** first operated the 707 on the New York to Los Angeles route in January 1959. Photographed at Newark, New Jersey in July 1970 is Boeing 707-323C N8417 (c/n 20089) being operated as a freighter. Sold on, it ended its days being used for spare parts for KC-135s at Davis-Monthan AFB in 1985. (Steve Williams)

TAP – Transportes Aereos Portugueses first operated the 707 on routes from Lisbon to South America in June 1966. Pictured at New York-JFK in July 1970 is Boeing 707-382B CS-TBG (c/n 20298). This aircraft was sold in Italy in 1988 and converted to a flying-tanker for the Italian Air Force where it still serves. (Ken Fielding)

Sudan Airways first introduced the 707 at the end of 1972. Pictured at London-Heathrow in July 1976 is Boeing 707-3J8C ST-AFB (c/n 20898). This aircraft is still in service with the company today but now in a freight configuration. (John Smith)

Although this 707 is in Saudia livery, it was in fact being operated by the **Saudi Arabian Royal Flight** as a VIP aircraft. Boeing 707-368C HZ-HM1 (c/n 21081) was at Paris-Charles de Gaulle in May 1977. In August 2003 it was reported to have been donated to a museum.

The Boeing 720 was shorter, by 9ft (2.74m), than the standard 707-100 series. Made from lighter gauge metal and with a reduced fuel capacity, its role was to fly short- to medium-haul routes. First flown in November 1959 it commenced operations with United Airlines the following July on the Los Angeles-Denver-Chicago service. Pictured at Vancouver, Canada in March 1973 is Boeing 720-047B N3165 (c/n 19438) of **Western Airlines**. This Los Angeles-based carrier was one of the oldest airlines in the USA, being able to trace its history back to 1925. In April 1987 it was merged into Delta Air Lines. This aircraft ended its days providing spares for KC-135s. (Ken Fielding)

The dominant carrier at the twin cities of Minneapolis-St Paul is **Northwest Airlines**. They received 720s in June 1961 for domestic services. Pictured at New York-JFK in July 1970 is Boeing 720-051B N733US (c/n 18384). This aircraft was sold on and is currently used as an engine testbed at Phoenix, Arizona. (Ken Fielding)

Air Rhodesia was formed by the government in September 1967. Since that regime was deemed by the United Nations to be an illegal one, services were only flown on domestic operations and to South Africa. Pictured at Johannesburg in May 1977 is VP-YNN Boeing 720-025 (c/n 18244). The airline became Air Zimbabwe in 1980 following independence. The aircraft was withdrawn from service in 1983, sold in 1988 and broken up for spares. (Bob O'Brien)

British holiday charter carrier **Monarch Airlines** took delivery of 720s in September 1971. They remained in service for twelve years. Pictured at Palma-Majorca in November 1973 is Boeing 720-051B G-AZNX (c/n 18383). The fate of this airframe was the common one for the type. It was to supply parts to KC-135s whilst being broken up at Davis-Monthan AFB.

Founded in 1973 as the national airline of Papua New Guinea, **Air Niugini** is government-owned. Pictured at Brisbane in November 1976 is Boeing 720-023B P2-ANG (c/n 18014). This airframe went to Davis-Monthan AFB to be broken up for spares. (Bob O'Brien)

Based in the capital Copenhagen, Danish carrier **Maersk Air** was formed in 1969, by a shipping company, to operate charter flights. Today they also fly scheduled passenger services. Their first 720 was delivered in September 1972 and they operated the type until 1981. Boeing 720-051B OY-APW (c/n 18422) is at Palma-Majorca in November 1973. Its fate was to supply KC-135 spares.

Avianca (Aerovias Nacionales de Colombia) is the Bogota-based national flag carrier for Colombia. It was formed in 1940 by a merger, but its roots go back to 1919 making it one of the oldest carriers in the world. Pictured at New York-JFK in July 1970 is Boeing 720-059B HK-726 (c/n 18831). This aircraft followed the trail to Davis-Monthan AFB to donate spares for KC-135s. (Ken Fielding)

By the end of the 1970s most of the 720s still in service had moved from the main to secondary carriers. One such was Boeing 720-022 N7224U (c/n 18077). Owned by **Sinclare Air Services** it had been fitted with an executive interior and was used for charter work. Pictured at Marana, Arizona in October 1979 it is in livery for a tour by the Bee Gees, a popular 1960s/70s rock music combo. The title on the cabin roof *Spirits having flown* refers to the latest disc being promoted. It is a pity that such a smart looking aircraft should end its days at Davis-Monthan AFB as spare parts for drab grey KC-135s.

The 1970s brought perhaps the most significant advance in passenger flying for the general public. This was the advent of the widebody airliner bringing affordable airfares to millions of people. The Lockheed company produced the L-1011 TriStar. Power was from three Rolls-Royce RB211 turbofans with a power output of 42,000 lb of static thrust each. The prototype first flew in November 1970 from Palmdale, California. Pictured on a sales mission to the Farnborough Air Show in September 1974 is TriStar 1 N10114 (c/n 1079) of **PSA – Pacific Southwest Airlines**. The carrier wanted to operate the aircraft on high-density routes in California such as Los Angeles to San Francisco. The airline was merged into US Air in 1988. This airframe was sold on to Canadian charter operator Worldways in 1985, eventually being broken up at Opa Locka, Florida in 1998.

Japanese carrier **All Nippon Airways** ordered their first TriStars in March 1971. The company used them on the very high-density domestic routes. L-1011 TriStar 1 JA8510 (c/n 1103) is at Tokyo-Haneda in May 1977. The aircraft was sold on in 1984 and is currently with Canadian airline Air Transat and for sale. (Bob O'Brien)

American carrier **TWA** was, with Eastern, the launch customer for the TriStar. They placed an order for 44 in March 1968. Their first service was in June 1972. Pictured at Los Angeles-LAX in October 1979 is L-1011 TriStar 1 N11003 (c/n 1015). This aircraft was retired by TWA at Kingman, Arizona in 1997.

Pictured landing at Farnborough in September 1972 is L-1011 TriStar 1 N305EA (c/n 1006). The aircraft is in basic Eastern Airlines livery, one of the joint launch customers, but has **BEA (British European Airways)** titles. The previous month BEA had ordered the type. By the time of the first delivery, in October 1974, BEA had merged with BOAC to become BA. This aircraft served with Eastern and then Delta before being stored at Mojave, California. It was broken up in 2002.

The TriStar 100 was a longer-range aircraft with increased gross weight and additional fuel tanks. Pictured at Paris-Charles de Gaulle in May 1977 is L-1011 TriStar 100 HZ-AHC (c/n 1137) of **Saudia**. This aircraft stayed with the carrier all its life; it was withdrawn from use in 1998 and offered for sale.

December 1974 saw **Gulf Air** order TriStars; they went on to operate 11 different aircraft. L-1011 TriStar 100 A4O-TW (c/n 1131) is at the carrier's Bahrain base in May 1977. Sold on this aircraft was converted to a freighter and is still in service with Miami-based Arrow Air. (Bob O'Brien)

The 500 series of the TriStar was the very long-range variant. It had higher output engines and a shorter, by 20ft 2in (6.14m), fuselage. The fuel capacity was increased and the range stretched to 5400nm (10,000km). L-1011 TriStar 500 G-BFCE (c/n 1168) of **British Airways** is at London-Heathrow in September 1979. This aircraft has since joined the Royal Air Force; it serves as a flying fuel tanker. (John Smith)

The first twin-aisle widebody from McDonnell Douglas was the DC-10. It outsold the TriStar with a production run of 446 (including the military KC-10) compared to 250 for the L-1011. The DC-10 first flew in August 1970 and was powered by three General Electric CF-6 turbofans of 39,300 lb static thrust. The launch customer was **American Airlines** who in February 1968 ordered fifty, half being options. They commenced operations with a service from Los Angeles to Chicago in August 1971. DC-10-10 N114AA (c/n 46514) is pictured at San Francisco in October 1979. This aircraft operated its entire life with AA and was retired to Amarillo, Texas in 1993, where it was broken up two years later.

United Airlines placed an order for thirty DC-10s with the same number of options in April 1968, services commenced in August 1971. DC-10-10 N1812U (c/n 46611) is pictured at San Francisco in October 1979. This aircraft has since been converted to a freight role and serves with major American parcel carrier FedEx.

British carrier **Laker Airways** ordered two DC-10s in anticipation of running its low-fare, no-reservation *Skytrain* service from London to New York. The first aircraft arrived in November 1972 but it was not until September 1977 that the *Skytrain* took off. In between, it operated holiday charters both European and transatlantic. DC-10-10 G-AZZC (c/n 46905) is pictured at Palma-Majorca in November 1973. Sadly Laker went into bankruptcy in February 1982. This aircraft was sold on and retired at Marana, Arizona in 1996: it was broken up the following year. (John Smith)

Miami-based **National Airlines** were the third carrier to put the DC-10 into service when, in December 1971, they flew from Florida to New York. At the start of the 1980s the company was taken over by Pan American. DC-10-10 N66NA (c/n 46708) is pictured at San Francisco in October 1979. This airframe was sold on to American Airlines in 1984, and now flies as a freighter for FedEx. (John Smith)

The first DC-10s **Thai Airways International** operated were leased and commenced services from Bangkok in April 1975. New aircraft from the manufacturer were delivered two years later. DC-10-30 HS-TGD (c/n 46959) is pictured departing London-Heathrow in June 1978. This aircraft was sold on in 1987 and is currently owned by Ghana Airways, which has it in store at Accra.

The -30 series DC-10 was the intercontinental version. It had extra fuel capacity, an enlarged wing and an additional centre fuselage undercarriage to help absorb the extra weight. Pictured at Manchester in May 1974 is DC-10-30CF N1032F (c/n 46826) of **ONA – Overseas National Airways**. This company was an American charter and contract carrier; they ceased operations in September 1978. This aircraft was destroyed by fire following a multiple birdstrike on take-off and overrunning the runway at New York-JFK in November 1975. (Ken Fielding)

Air New Zealand's first DC-10 was delivered in January 1973 and initially used across the Tasman Sea to Sydney in Australia. DC-10-30 ZK-NZS (c/n 46954) is at Los Angeles-LAX in October 1976. This aircraft was sold on and is currently in store at Havana, Cuba. (Steve Williams)

Oakland, California-based **Trans International Airlines** ordered three DC-10s in 1968 and they flew their first widebody charter in May 1973. In 1979 they were renamed Transamerica Airlines and then suspended all services in September 1986. Pictured at London-Gatwick in August 1973 is DC-10-30CF N102TV (c/n 46801). This airframe flies today as a parcel carrier for FedEx in the USA. (John Smith)

Belgian flag carrier **Sabena's** first revenue flight with the DC-10 was across the Atlantic in November 1973. Pictured at Tokyo-Haneda in May 1977 is DC-10-30CF OO-SLA (c/n 47906). The airline ceased services in 2001 and this aircraft currently operates for an African cargo company. (Bob O'Brien)

Pictured at Tokyo-Haneda in May 1977 is DC-10-30 HB-IHB (c/n 46576) of **Swissair**. The carrier was the first to operate the type across the Atlantic when they flew Zurich to Montreal in December 1972. Swissair ceased operations in 2001. This aircraft was sold on in 1986, retired in 2002 and then broken up. (Bob O'Brien)

The -40 series DC-10 was a -30 powered by Pratt & Whitney JT9D turbofans with a power output of 47,000 lb static thrust. **Japan Air Lines** was one of only two customers to specify the type. DC-10-40 JA8532 (c/n 46660) is at Tokyo-Haneda in May 1977. This aircraft still serves with JAL. (Bob O'Brien)

The most successful of all the widebody airliners has been the Boeing 747, known worldwide as the 'Jumbo Jet'. It was first flown in February 1969 and the latest variant, the -400 series, is still in production. Launch customer was **Pan American**. Pictured at San Francisco in October 1979 is Boeing 747-121 N754PA (c/n 19658). This aircraft was sold on in 1986 to Cargolux, and later Corsair, before being retired at Mojave, California in 1995.

The 747 became almost a 'must have' aircraft for airlines around the world. Most international carriers operated some on their most prestigious routes. Pictured at New York-JFK in July 1970 is Boeing 747-131 N93105 (c/n 19671) of **Trans World Airways**. Only four months old at that time, it went on to have a long career with the carrier serving solely them until 1994 when it was retired. It was broken up at Kansas City six years later.

Showing its classic livery is **Air France** Boeing 747-128 N28903 (c/n 20541) at Paris-Charles de Gaulle in May 1977. This aircraft has been preserved since February 2000 by the Musée de l'Air at Paris-Le Bourget.

United Airlines Boeing 747-122 N4727U (c/n 19883) is pictured departing San Francisco in October 1979. The carrier operated this aircraft all its life, from delivery in June 1972 until retirement in September 1996. It was then used for spares reclamation.

Pictured at San Francisco in October 1979 is **American Airlines** Boeing 747-123 N9667 (c/n 20106). This aircraft was sold on in 1984, withdrawn and stored in 1999, before being broken up the following year at Greenwood, Mississippi.

Aer Lingus – Irish International Airlines Boeing 747-148 EI-ASJ (c/n 19745) is pictured landing at the company's Dublin base in July 1971. The aircraft had been delivered just four months earlier and, apart from a spell on lease to British Airways, stayed with them into the 1990s. It went to Nigerian operator Kabo Air and was then retired to Roswell, New Mexico. (Steve Williams)

Japan Air Lines Boeing 747-146A JA8128 (c/n 21029) is pictured departing London-Heathrow in June 1978. This aircraft served the carrier until August 2003 when it was sold to Orient Thai.

British Airways have operated 747s from the earliest days and currently have a large fleet of -400 series aircraft. Boeing 747-136 G-AWNM (c/n 20708) is pictured crew training at Prestwick in October 1976. It was operated all its life by the carrier before being retired and stored in New Mexico at the end of 1999.

The -200 series 747 featured extra fuel capacity and a greater take-off weight. Pictured at London-Heathrow in June 1978 is Boeing 747-2B4B OD-AGJ (c/n 21099) of Beirut-based **MEA – Middle East Airlines**. This aircraft was sold on, converted to a freighter in 1998, and currently serves with US carrier Kalitta Air.

Pictured at Manchester in August 1977 is Boeing 747-217B C-FCRE (c/n 20929) of **CP Air**. This aircraft was sold in Pakistan during 1985, retired, and stored at Karachi at the end of 2002. (John Smith)

El Al Boeing 747-258B 4X-AXA (c/n 20135) is seen at London-Heathrow in June 1978. The flag carrier for Israel operated this aircraft for its entire life, from delivery in May 1971 until retirement in 1999.

Pictured at Perth in November 1976 is Boeing 747-238B VH-EBC (c/n 20011) of Australian carrier Qantas. It is in the airline's original livery for the type. It was sold on in 1984 and eventually retired and broken up at New York in 2000. (Bob O'Brien)

World Airways Boeing 747-273C N748WA (c/n 20652) is seen at Manchester in March 1974. Over the years this aircraft has been leased to many carriers. It was withdrawn from use in 2000 at Marana, Arizona and partly dismantled. (Ken Fielding)

Photographed at Los Angeles-LAX in October 1979 is Boeing 747-230B HL7442 (c/n 20559) of **Korean Air Lines**. This aircraft was the centre of a major diplomatic incident when it was operating flight number KE007 on September 1st 1983. During its route from the west coast of the USA to Korea it was shot down into the Okhotsk Sea by a Soviet Air Force Sukhoi Su-15 from Sokol Airfield on Sakhalin Island. The reason for it being in the wrong place remains a mystery, the many theories ranging from crew error to spying.

Founded in 1946 as Seaboard and Western, the name changed to **Seaboard World Airlines** in 1961. The company was a scheduled cargo carrier which merged with Federal Express in 1980. Pictured at London-Heathrow in June 1978 is Boeing 747-245F N701SW (c/n 20826). This variant is an all-cargo aircraft with an upward-opening nose cargo door and no cabin windows. This aircraft was sold on and is currently in store at Stansted, UK as G-INTL of Air Freight Express. (John Smith)

One of the most distinctive liveries of any carrier had to be that of Dallas-based **Braniff Airways**, which painted its 747s orange. The company ceased operations and re-started several times, but flies no more. Pictured at Los Angeles-LAX in October 1979 is Boeing 747-227B N607BN (c/n 22234). Sold on, this aircraft is currently owned by Northwest Airlines and is in store at Marana, Arizona. (John Smith)

First flown in July 1974, the 747SP (Special Performance) was a very long-range -100 series with a 48ft (14.63m) shorter fuselage. Only 45 aircraft were built. Pictured at London-Heathrow in July 1976 is **Pan American** Boeing 747SP-21 N533PA (c/n 21025). Sold to United Airlines, it ended its days in Oklahoma where it was broken up for spare parts in 1995. (John Smith)

Seen at London-Heathrow in June 1978 is Boeing 747SP-86 EP-IAC (c/n 21093) of **Iran Air**. This aircraft was ordered by the carrier in 1974, delivered in 1977 and is still in service today.

Few jet airliners have been so obviously derived from a bomber as Russia's Tupolev Tu-104. It first flew in June 1955 having been developed from the Tu-16 (NATO reporting name *Badger*). Power came from a pair of 14,880 lb thrust Mikulin RD-3 turbojets. Following the Comet it was the second pure jet airliner to enter service, and the first in the short to medium-haul role.

Pictured at Amsterdam-Schiphol in July 1970 is Tupolev Tu-104A CCCP-42397 (c/n 9350902) of **Aeroflot**. In the days of the Soviet Union all civil aircraft, from crop sprayers to international airliners, were in Aeroflot livery. This aircraft was cancelled from the Russian register in 1978 and presumably scrapped.

In America there was the Lockheed Electra, in the UK the Bristol Britannia, whilst in Russia they had the Ilyushin IL-18. All were turboprop-powered in the days when passengers wanted pure jets. This meant that the two western designs had relatively short lives with the major airlines, albeit long ones with secondary carriers. In the Soviet bloc 'passenger appeal' or 'passenger choice' were not phrases on the lips of Aeroflot and the airlines of the communist satellites. This gave the IL-18 a bigger production run and a longer service life. The design first flew in 1957 and was powered by four Kuznetsov NK-4 turboprops of 4000shp or Ivchenko AI-20s of 3755shp. Pictured at Manchester in June 1970 is Ilyushin IL-18V LZ-BEP (c/n 185008105) of Bulgarian flag carrier **TABSO**. The airline was renamed Balkan Bulgarian and this aircraft was damaged beyond repair after a landing accident in the Yemen in June 1984. (Ken Fielding)

Pictured at Paris-Le Bourget in May 1971 is Ilyushin IL-18V TZ-ABE (c/n 181003304) of **Air Mali**. This airline was the national carrier from the African republic of Mali. The Bamako-based company suspended operations in 1988. This airframe crashed in Upper Volta in August 1974.

First flown in July 1963, the Tupolev Tu-134 was a short-haul airliner powered by a pair of Soloviev D-30 turbofans with a power output of 14,990 lb of static thrust. Over 850 were constructed for use by Aeroflot and Russia's client states. Pictured at Manchester in September 1979 is Tu-134A YU-AJD (c/n 2351508) of **Aviogenex**. The Belgrade-based carrier now operates a fleet of western-built jets. This aircraft was returned to Russia, operated by Aeroflot in the 1990s and later by Knaapo at Komsomolsk in a combi role. (John Smith)

As Poland has embraced the west following the demise of the USSR and the Warsaw Pact, the state airline **LOT (Polskie Linie Lotnicze)** has been quick to dump all its old Russian-built 'gas-guzzlers' for newer American and Brazilian-built airliners. Pictured at London-Heathrow in June 1978 is Tupolev Tu-134A SP-LHB (c/n 3531809). This aircraft has been preserved at the Krakow museum. (John Smith)

Pictured at Glasgow in October 1976 is Tupolev Tu-134A CCCP-65021 (c/n 48390) in the colours of Soviet airline **Aeroflot**. The aircraft was at the time being operated in a VIP role and had brought a high-level delegation to visit. It went on to serve in the autonomous republic of Tatarstan and with a Moscow-based carrier in 2002.

First flown in October 1968, the Tupolev Tu-154 was a scaled-up Tu-134. Power was from three Kuznetsov NK-8 turbofans all tail-mounted. Production ran to over 900 airframes. Pictured at Manchester in September 1979 is Tu-154 HA-LCL (c/n 73A-051) of Hungarian national carrier **MALEV**. This was the last Tu-154 operated by the carrier; it was returned to Russia in 1980 and cancelled from the register. (John Smith)

The Tu-154B had greater passenger capacity, extra doors and more modern flight controls. Pictured at Paris-Le Bourget in June 1977 is Tupolev Tu-154B CCCP-85207 (c/n 77A-207) in the colours of **Aeroflot**. This aircraft was cancelled from the Russian register in June 1998.

The Ilyushin IL-76 is a heavy transport aircraft powered by four Soloviev D-30KP turbofans with an output of 26,455 lb of static thrust. Pictured at Paris-Le Bourget in June 1977 is IL-76 CCCP-76500 (c/n 01014) in the colours of **Aeroflot**. This airframe was withdrawn and broken up at Zhukovsky by the mid 1990s.

The Ilyushin IL-62 is a long-range airliner powered by four rear-mounted Kuznetsov NK-8 turbofans with an output of 23,150 lbst each. The prototype first flew in January 1961. Pictured at London-Heathrow in June 1978 is IL-62 OK-DBE (c/n 31501) of **CSA (Ceskoslovenske Aerolinie)**. Following the peaceful split of the Czech and Slovak republics the carrier is now known as CSA Czech Airlines. This aircraft was withdrawn from use at the end of 1988. (John Smith)

In the Soviet Union they also had a need for a turboprop to replace vast numbers of piston-engined airliners, in their case Ilyushin IL-12 and IL-14s, still in service. The Antonov Design Bureau produced, in the An-24, the first of a long line of aircraft. First flown in December 1959 it was powered by a pair of Ivchenko AI-24 turboprops. Pictured at Liverpool-Speke in February 1974 is Antonov An-24B YR-AMP (c/n 77303505) of Romanian government-owned carrier **TAROM**. This Bucharest-based airline now has a fleet of American and European-built aircraft. The registration of this aircraft was cancelled in December 1978 following a reported crash. (Ian Keast)

One of the largest freight aircraft ever built was the Antonov An-22. It first flew in February 1965 and was powered by four Kuznetsov NK-12 turboprops each producing a massive 15,000shp. Pictured at Paris-Le Bourget in May 1977 is An-22 CCCP-09316 (c/n 01340308) in the livery of **Aeroflot**. This aircraft has since appeared in Russian Air Force markings.

The 1970s saw another significant event in civil aviation. This was the entry into service of the first European-built Airbus aircraft. The first type in service was the A300, this commenced operations with **Air France** in May 1974 on the Paris to London route. Pictured at Heathrow in June 1978 is Airbus A300B2-100 F-BVGF (c/n 013). This airframe was retired during 1996, in Oklahoma, and broken up.

Greek flag carrier **Olympic Airways** received its first Airbus widebodies in February 1979. Pictured at London-Heathrow, in September of that year, is Airbus A300B4-102 SX-BEC (c/n 056). This aircraft was retired and broken up at Greensboro in 1998. (John Smith)

With a total production run of just twelve aircraft, including prototypes, the Dassault Mercure was one of the great failures of any airliner in modern times. It first flew in May 1971 and was used by only one airline: **Air Inter**. Mercure 100 F-BTMD (c/n 02) is pictured on a sales tour at San Francisco in October 1976. This aircraft was later delivered to Air Inter, withdrawn, stored and then broken up at Paris-Orly in 1992. (Steve Williams)

Sikorsky S-58ET G-BCLN (c/n 581539) was flying North Sea oil industry support missions for **British Airways Helicopters** when photographed at Shetland Airport in December 1975. The company became British International Helicopters in 1986 while the aircraft now does aerial work for a Detroit-Willow Run operator. (Bob O'Brien)

Founded in 1949, **New York Airways** became in 1953 the first helicopter airline. It linked downtown Manhattan with the city's airports. Sikorsky S-61L N617PA (c/n 61425) is pictured at New York-JFK in July 1970. The carrier ceased operations in the early part of 1979 and this aircraft is current with a California-based company. (Ken Fielding)

UK-based **Bristow Helicopters** operates worldwide support to offshore gas and oil installations. Bell 212 G-BCMC (c/n 30639) is seen hovering at Aberdeen-Dyce in September 1977. From this location North Sea oil platforms are serviced. This aircraft was sold in Spain during 1999 where it still operates.

The Aerospatiale/BAC Concorde was the ultimate head-turning aeroplane. It was so well known that it was never referred to as 'a Concorde' or 'the Concorde'… it was just 'Concorde'. British Airways and Air France both started commercial services on 21st January 1976: BA operating to Bahrain and Air France to Rio de Janeiro via Dakar. Pictured at London-Heathrow in June 1978 is Concorde 102 G-BOAC (c/n 204) of **British Airways**. The fleet was retired in October 2003 and this aircraft is now on display at Manchester Airport.

Russia put its SST into service at the end of 1975: before Concorde, but only on cargo services from Moscow to Alma Ata. Passenger operations did not start until two years later; these only lasted until June 1978. Pictured at Paris-Le Bourget in June 1977 is Tupolev Tu-144 CCCP-77110 (c/n 06-1) in the livery of **Aeroflot**. This aircraft is now preserved at the Museum of Civil Aviation in Ulyanovsk.

Index of Airlines

Bibliography

Books

Airlife's Commercial Aircraft & Airliners: Rod Simpson; Airlife.

The Boeing 707, 720 and C-135: Tony Pither; Air Britain.

Jet Airliner Production List Volume 1 & 2 (various editions): Tony Eastwood & John Roach; The Aviation Hobby Shop.

JP Airline Fleets: Ulrich Klee; Bucher & Co, Zürich (various editions).

Lockheed L-1011 TriStar: Philip Birtles; Airlife.

McDonnell Douglas DC-10: Gunter Endres; Airlife.

Piston Engine Airliner Production List (various editions): Tony Eastwood & John Roach; The Aviation Hobby Shop.

Turbo Prop Airliner Production List (various editions): Tony Eastwood & John Roach; The Aviation Hobby Shop.

Magazines

Airliner World, Airliners, Airways, Aviation Letter, International Air Power Review & Propliner (various editions).

We hope you enjoyed this book . . .

Midland Publishing offers an extensive range of outstanding aviation titles, of which a small selection are shown here.

We always welcome ideas from authors or readers for books they would like to see published.

In addition, our associate, Midland Counties Publications, offers an exceptionally wide range of aviation, military, naval and transport books and videos for sale by mail-order worldwide.

For a copy of the appropriate catalogue, or to order further copies of this book, and any other Midland Publishing titles, please write, telephone, fax or e-mail to:

Midland Counties Publications
4 Watling Drive, Hinckley,
Leics, LE10 3EY, England
Tel: (+44) 01455 254 450
Fax: (+44) 01455 233 737
E-mail: midlandbooks@compuserve.com
www.midlandcountiessuperstore.com

US distribution by Specialty Press –
see page 2.

1000 CIVIL AIRCRAFT IN COLOUR

Gerry Manning

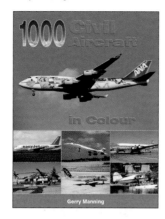

From Air Alfa to Zoom Airlines, here are photographs of civil airliners and other transport types, both large and small. Captured worldwide in recent years, they display a multiplicity of markings as they go about tasks ranging from international schedules to obscure freight operations. Extended captions detail type, individual aircraft, operator and location. Additional features include BA's fast-disappearing 'World Images' colours and aircraft in eye-catching special or promotional colour schemes.

Softback, 280 x 215 mm, 160 pages
over 1,000 full colour photographs
1 85780 208 X **£18.99**

ARRIVALS & DEPARTURES
North American Airlines 1990-2000

John K Morton

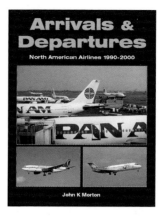

This is a photographic record, with extended captions, of new and departed North American airlines during the last decade of the 20th century. It is divided into three sections: 'Arrivals' contains 32 airlines which began operations during the period and were still operational at the end of it; 'Arrivals and Departures' features 24 carriers which came and went, and 'Departures' covers 29 airlines which went out of business in the 1990s. Included here are famous names such as PanAm, Eastern and Tower Air.

Softback, 280 x 215 mm, 112 pages
168 full colour photographs
1 85780 200 4 **£14.99**

EUROPEAN AIRLINES

John K Morton

This book portrays with extended captions, a broad selection of over 100 primarily passenger-carrying airlines from 33 European countries. Starting in Ireland and continuing around the continent, the reader is taken on a 'tour' of European nations, and in each case liveries of based airlines, including all the major flag carriers, scheduled and charter airlines are included. As wide a variety of types – jets and propliners – as possible are shown and an equally-varied range of colour schemes.

Softback, 280 x 215 mm, 112 pages
188 full colour photographs
1 85780 210 1 **£14.99**

AIRLINERS WORLDWIDE
Over 100 Current Airliners Described and Illustrated in Colour (2nd edition)

Tom Singfield

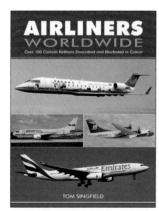

The coverage in this new edition of this valuable guidebook is markedly different, up-to-the-minute and indispensible. The text for each type has been revised and updated. Each type has an historical narrative and description of model variants and type of operations plus principal technical details and a listing of current operators. The photographic selection is all new and types new to this edition include the Embraer 170 and 195, the Antonov An-140, Airbus A318 and A380.

Softback, 240 x 170 mm, 128 pages
136 colour photographs
1 85780 189 X **£13.99**

AIRLINES REMEMBERED
Over 200 Airlines of the Past, Described and Illustrated in Colour

B I Hengi

In the same format as the enormously popular *Airlines Worldwide* and *Airliners Worldwide*, this companion reviews the histories and operations of over 200 airlines from the last thirty years which are no longer with us, each illustrated with a full colour photograph showing at least one of their aircraft in the colour scheme of that era. Operators such as BEA, CP Air, Eastern, Invicta, Jet 24, Laker and Fred Olsen are examples of the extensive and varied coverage.

Softback, 240 x 170 mm, 224 pages
c200 colour photographs
1 85780 091 5 **£14.95**

THE GENERAL AVIATION HANDBOOK (3rd Edition)

Rod Simpson

A single point of reference for everyone with an interest in the lighter side of aviation, this guide to post-war general aviation manufacturers and the aircraft they have produced is extensively illustrated in colour. Model-by-model tabular listings of the larger producers give detailed information on the differences between variants and the numbers that were built. From executive jets to the many new ultralight designs exploiting composite materials, there is something to be learnt on every page.

Softback, 280 x 215 mm, c320 pages
over 500 mostly colour photographs
1 85780 222 5 c**£29.99**

RUSSIAN AIRLINES AND THEIR AIRCRAFT

Dmitriy Komissarov &
Yefim Gordon

Following the ending of Aeroflot's monopoly in 1992 and the break-up of the Soviet Union, the Russian civil air transport scene has been considerably transformed.

This full-colour album covers the major airlines operating in Russia today, illustrating the types operated by each carrier, their equipment and the various colour schemes worn by them. A brief history and fleet information are provided for each airline, as are detailed photo captions.

Softback, 280 x 215 mm, 160 pages
449 full colour photographs
1 85780 176 8 **£19.99**